KU-826-701

Paul of
Jul of Organisational
Behaviour

Organizational Behavior

Volume 8
EMPLOYEE VERSUS OWNER ISSUES
IN ORGANIZATIONS

Trends in Organizational Behavior

Volume 8
EMPLOYEE VERSUS OWNER ISSUES IN ORGANIZATIONS

Edited by

Cary L. Cooper

Manchester School of Management, University of Manchester Institute of
Science and Technology, UK

and

Denise M. Rousseau

Carnegie Mellon University, Pittsburgh, USA

JOHN WILEY & SONS, LTD
Chichester · New York · Weinheim · Brisbane · Singapore · Toronto

Other Wiley Editorial Offices

John Wiley & Sons, Inc., 605 Third Avenue,
New York, NY 10158-0012, USA

Wiley-VCH Verlag GmbH, Pappelallee 3,
D-69469 Weinheim, Germany

John Wiley & Sons Australia Ltd, 33 Park Road, Milton,
Queensland 4064, Australia

John Wiley & Sons (Asia) Pte Ltd, 2 Clementi Loop #02-01,
Jin Xing Distripark, Singapore 129809

John Wiley & Sons (Canada) Ltd, 22 Worcester Road,
Rexdale, Ontario M9W 1L1, Canada

British Library Cataloguing in Publication Data

A catalogue record for this book is available from the British Library

ISBN 0-471-49854-8

Typeset in 10/12 pt Palatino by Dorwyn Ltd, Rowlands Castle, Hants.
Printed and bound in Great Britain by Bookcraft (Bath) Ltd, Midsomer Norton.
This book is printed on acid-free paper responsibly manufactured from sustainable
forestry, in which at least two trees are planted for each one used in paper production.

Contents

About the Editors

CARY L. COOPER

Cary L. Cooper is currently BUPA Professor of Organizational Psychology and Health in the Manchester School of Management, and Deputy Vice-Chancellor (External Activities) of the University of Manchester Institute of Science and Technology (UMIST). He is the author of over 80 books (on occupational stress, women at work, and industrial and organizational psychology), has written over 300 scholarly articles for academic journals, and is a frequent contributor to national newspapers, TV and radio. He is currently Founding Editor of the *Journal of Organizational Behavior*, co-Editor of the medical journal *Stress Medicine*; Co-editor of the *International Journal of Management Review*. He is a Fellow of the British Psychological Society, The Royal Society of Arts, The Royal Society of Medicine and the Royal Society of Health. Professor Cooper is the President of the British Academy of Management, is a Companion of the (British) Institute of Management and one of the first UK based Fellows of the (American) Academy of Management (having also won the 1998 Distinguished Service Award for his contribution to management science from the Academy of Management). Professor Cooper is the Editor (jointly with Professor Chris Argyris of Harvard Business School) of the international scholarly *Blackwell Encyclopedia of Management* (12 volume set). He has been an advisor to the World Health Organization, ILO, and recently published a major report for the EU's European Foundation for the Improvement of Living and Work Conditions on 'Stress Prevention in the Workplace'.

DENISE M. ROUSSEAU

Denise Rousseau H. J. Heinz II Professor of Organizational Behavior and Public Policy at Carnegie Mellon University, jointly in the Heinz School of Public Policy and Management and in the Graduate School of Industrial

Administration. She has been a faculty member at Northwestern University, the University of Michigan, and the Naval Postgraduate School.

Her research addresses the impact of work group processes on performance and the changing psychological contract at work. Rousseau is an author of more than 80 articles which have appeared in prominent academic journals, such as the *Journal of Applied Psychology, Academy of Management Review*, and *Administrative Science Quarterly*. She is currently Editor-in-Chief of the *Journal of Organizational Behavior*. Her other books include: *Psychological Contracts in Organizations: Understanding Written and Unwritten Agreements* (Sage); the *Trends in Organizational Behavior* series (Wiley) with Cary Cooper, *Developing an Interdisciplinary Science of Organizations* (Jossey-Bass) with Karlene Roberts and Charles Hulin; *The Boundaryless Career* (Oxford) with Michael Arthur; *Psychological Contracts in Employment: Cross-National Perspectives* (Sage) with Rene Schalk; and *Relational Wealth* (Oxford) with Carrie Leana.

Professor Rousseau has consulted in diverse organizations and written numerous articles for managers and executives including "Teamwork: inside and out" (*Business Week/Advance*), "Managing diversity for high performance" (*Business Week/Advance*) and "Two ways to change (and keep) the psychological contract" (*Academy of Management Executive*). She has taught in executive programs at Northwestern (Kellogg), Cornell, Carnegie Mellon and in industry programs for health care, journalism and manufacturing among others.

She is a Fellow in the American Psychological Association, Society for Industrial and Organizational Psychology, and the Academy of Management.

List of Contributors

Joseph Blasi	Rutgers University, School of Management and Labor Relations, Rockafeller Road, Levin Building, New Brunswick, NJ 08903, USA
Annette Cox	Manchester School of Management, University of Manchester Institute of Science and Technology, PO Box 88, Manchester, M60 1QD, UK
Claudia J. Ferrante	Heinz School, Carnegie Mellon University, Pittsburgh, PA 15213, USA
Jerome A. Katz	Saint Louis University, Cook School, 3674 Lindell Blvd, St. Louis, MO 63108, USA
Douglas Kruse	Rutgers University, School of Management and Labor Relations, Rockafeller Road, Levin Building, New Brunswick, NJ 08903, USA
Marc Orlitzky	Australian Graduate School of Management, University of New South Wales, Sydney, NSW 2052, Australia
Denise M. Rousseau	Heinz School, Carnegie Mellon University, Pittsburgh, PA 15213, USA
Sara L. Rynes	College of Business Admin, W252 PBAB, The University of Iowa, Iowa City, IA 52242-1000, USA
Zipi Shperling	The Leon Recanati Graduate School of Business Administration, Tel Aviv University, Tel Aviv 69978, Israel
Paul Sparrow	Management School, University of Sheffield, 9 Mappin Street, Sheffield S1 4DT, UK
Pamela M. Williams	Saint Louis University, Cook School, 3674 Lindell Blvd, St. Louis, MO 63108, USA

Editorial Introduction

This issue of Trends in Organizational Behavior explores the theme of employee versus owner issues. As more and more large organizations downsize, as employees set up their own businesses or work increasingly for small and medium sized enterprises, and as the psychological contract between employee and employer in larger organizations is undermined, the issues around employee involvement and ownership become very important. All of these issues are explored in this volume, with topics on employee equity, share ownership for workers, the psychological consequences of firm ownership, employee loyalty, achieving ownership of performance, open book management and employee stock transfers in SMEs.

We draw on the expertise for these topics once again from a group of distinguished academics who are at the forefront of this important field.

We hope the focus of this volume will help to stimulate further research in this twenty-first-century trend in organizational behaviour.

DMR
CLC

CHAPTER 1

Employee Equity: Employee versus Owner Issues in Organizational Behavior

Joseph R. Blasi and Douglas L. Kruse
School of Management and Labor Relations, Rutgers University, USA

INTRODUCTION

What are the cutting edge organizational behavior issues in the arena of employee share ownership? Because we are most familiar with data and trends in the United States, the US employee equity sector will be our focus. Initially, the cutting edge issues cannot be assessed without first examining the incidence of various employee share plans. If employee share plans are an insubstantial part of modern capitalist society, then the issues that will most concern us will be theoretical questions. (For a review of such questions, see Blair, Kruse & Blasi 2000.) If that is the case, then this discussion can simply continue the debates about whether employee share ownership can work in capitalist societies. This debate was essentially started by the English scholars Sidney and Beatrice Webb in the previous century (Webb 1987). Next, we will explore the empirical evidence on organizational behavior issues. Significant research has now taken place in the United States on real cases of employee share ownership and a rich research literature exists. Unfortunately, both the existence of and the conclusions from this literature have not made their way into mainstream organizational behavior discussions. We will then briefly review the available research on what workers actually think. Lastly, we will mention a few key questions for organization behavior scholars.

Trends in Organizational Behavior, Volume 8. Edited by C. L. Cooper and D. M. Rousseau.
© 2001 John Wiley & Sons, Ltd.

EMPLOYEE EQUITY: THE INCIDENCE

There are a variety of forms that employee equity can take. Oddly enough, because of the strange taxonomy that law and public practice has assigned to these many forms, there is little comprehensive understanding among organizational behavior specialists of the whole picture. Thus, while most scholars can describe the incidence of self-directed work teams, few can describe the incidence of employee equity programs. This may not have been an important deficit in the past. However, now that these programs represent a significant alteration in capitalism, clear understanding by scholars is more important.

Employee Stock Ownership Plans

In the United States, since the 1970s, the main vehicle for employee ownership has historically been the Employee Stock Ownership Plan (ESOP), which was first given recognition and special tax treatment as a form of pension plan in the 1974 ERISA law. The ESOP is basically a retirement trust that invests its assets mainly in securities of the employer of workers. It is important to understand that workers typically do not use their own money to gain employee ownership through ESOPs. It is provided to them as an employee benefit by employers who get tax incentives for doing so. In the United States, companies can borrow funds from banks to set up ESOPs. These are called leveraged ESOPs and typically are used to buy large chunks of a firm's stock in one single transaction. As the firm pays off the loan slowly, the shares are credited to the individual accounts of the workers. For example, leveraged ESOPs are used to accomplish employee buyouts. (The operation of ESOPs is explained at the National Center for Employee Ownership's (NCEO) web site at www.nceo.org.) There are currently about 7.2 million participants, representing 7.0 per cent of the private-sector workforce, in over 9200 ESOPs with combined assets of US$263 billion (US DOL 1999, p. 56). The NCEO estimates that only about 2000 of these ESOPs have majority ownership in the corporation. These ESOPs are in both publicly traded stock market companies, like United Airlines, and closely held corporations.[1] Among large public companies, only a few are majority employee-owned (United Airlines most prominently), but among public companies generally (where the SEC defines a 5 per cent stockholder as a major stakeholder) almost 1000 have more than 4 per cent of stock held broadly by employees, with average employee holdings of 12 per cent (Blasi & Kruse 1991). There has been

---

[1] Estimate made by Corey Rosen of the National Center for Employee Ownership, Oakland, CA.

substantial growth of public firms with more than 20 per cent of broad employee ownership (Blair, Kruse & Blasi 2000). The NCEO provides an annual list of the main examples of significant employee ownership in public and private companies. Most majority employee ownership is in closely held firms. While a large number of US employees own employer stock, almost all of this stock is in firms that are minority employee-owned. This is mainly the result of successful family businesses selling out to the employees in employee buyouts after the family founder decides to retire. Only occasionally do these sales of family businesses involve a worker buyout of a failing firm or the worker buyout of a unionized firm. The NCEO has identified scores of closely-held corporations cutting across all industries in the United States in the 30–50 per cent ownership range.

401k/Deferred Profit-sharing Plans

Apart from ESOPs, there are just over eight million participants in non-ESOP defined contribution pension plans that hold employer stock, which hold a total of $91 billion of employer stock (over 80 per cent in 401(k) plans).[2] The 401(k) plan is a common form of retirement plan where employees make contributions—which are often matched by employers—to a retirement trust account and then invest the assets in this account in various stocks, bonds, and money market investments, including the stock of their employer. If the employee ownership in these plans is mainly as a result of employee contributions, then it is really employee ownership bought by the employees. However, in the United States, many retirement accounts called deferred profit-sharing trusts actually use deferred profit-sharing payments from the firm mainly to invest in employer stock in such retirement accounts and hence they are really like employee ownership plans. Where a deferred profit-sharing trust uses company profit-sharing payments to invest in its own stock, this is employee ownership purchased by the firm. (The operation of these benefit plans is discussed at the website of the Profit Sharing/401(k) Council of America at http://www.psca.org/.) Some studies suggest that as much as 20 per cent of the assets of this popular form of retirement saving may be in employer stock.[3] With existing data it is difficult to determine the

---

[2] These and the other figures in this section are based on calculations by the authors from the US Department of Labor's Pension and Welfare Benefits Administration's Form 5500 data for fiscal years 1994 and 1995, which are the most recent complete data available.

[3] The average percent of 401k plans assets invested in company stock in 1993 was 1.1 per cent for plans with 500 or fewer participants, 3.1 per cent for 501–1000 participants, 6.4 per cent for 1001–5000 participants, and 15.3 per cent for more than 5000 participants (Kroumova 1999). More recently, a study by the Employee Benefit Research Institute and the Investment Company Institute found that for all participants as of 1996, 19.1 per cent is invested in employer stock (Investment Company Institute 1999).

distribution of workers with differing amounts of retirement funds in company shares, and different analysts may disagree about what percentage might fall under the rubric of invested 'substantially'. Freeman & Dube (2000) guestimate that the proportion with substantial investments could be as high as 11 per cent.

Employee Stock Purchase Plans

Employees may purchase and own stock directly in their companies through stock purchase programs, which was done by 8.9 per cent of employees in 1983 (Brickley & Hevert 1991). Employee share purchase plans are offered in 42 per cent of large US public corporations and typically allow employees to buy an upper limit of shares in their company at a 15 per cent discount to the public stock market price with the employer absorbing brokerage fees. Recent national data on employee share purchase plans indicate they own about one per cent of public market stock. A recent study of employee share purchase plans focusing on the largest 100 pure Internet public companies by market value in the United States has established that the average ownership of these companies by employees is between 0.5 and 1 per cent. Given the small number of employees in these firms and their huge market value, this represents substantial wealth (Blasi & Kruse 2000).

Stock Option Programs

Employees may gain an equity interest in their company by participating in company offered stock option programs. Until the early 1990s it was hard to find more than a handful of public corporations that offered stock options more broadly than to their top executives and key managers. New estimates from the NCEO indicate that between seven and ten million employees actually receive stock options in the United States. Among the well-known companies giving options to most or all employees are Starbucks, Amazon.com, Bristol-Myers Squibb, Procter & Gamble, and Microsoft. The NCEO numbers are based in part on information from the Bureau of Labor Statistics, the American Electronics Association, the Center for Effective Organizations at the University of Southern California, and multiple surveys from various compensation consultants (NCEO 2000). In the 1990s all-employee stock option programs, in which stock options are given to most or all employees, have grown rapidly. These exist in three per cent of all large New York stock exchange companies. Recent surveys by the US Federal Reserve Board suggest that as many as one-third of large corporations have stock option plans for all or most of their employees.[4] These sources suggest that broad-based stock option programs that include most workers are ubiquitous in high techology and Internet companies, as they spread to old economy firms. (For a focus on these firms, see www.fed.org.) Some estimates suggest that these options would represent upwards of 20 per cent of the fully diluted equity of most of these firms if they were all exercised today! (Blasi et al. 2000; Investor Responsibility Research Center 1998).

Worker Cooperatives

Workers may also own their companies as members of worker cooperatives (Jones 1979; Bonin, Jones & Putterman 1993). The efficacy of worker cooperatives as a third way between capitalism and socialism was the inspiration of the debates about employee equity and organization initiated by Sidney and Beatrice Webb a century ago.

Thus, while these measurements indicate reasonable diffusion, the important insights into whether employee equity is a meaningful trend in American society come from a series of recent national surveys of adults. Until recently, researchers have focused on case studies of different individual companies or estimates of the individual incidence of these different forms of employee ownership using databases particular to each one. The presumption has been that employee equity is a minor organizational phenomenon. But national random surveys allow us to account for the fact that most firms that have employee equity programs have several types of these programs. Only recently has a definitive national picture emerged with the availability of the results of a wide variety of national representative surveys of adults in the 1990s by public polling firms that asked about participation in employee equity programs. (For a detailed review of these new data see Kruse & Blasi 1999.) Combining the various methods of owning employer stock and adjusting for overlap, 20–25 per cent of American adults report holding stock in the company in which they work.[5]

The implications of employee share ownership for future organizational studies can be assessed further by looking more broadly at two other types of shared capitalism approaches, namely profit sharing and gain sharing. About one-fifth of US employees participate in some type of profit sharing, while just under one-third of US firms have profit-sharing

---

[4] On the basis of a survey of 415 companies in its 12 regions, the Fed estimates that a third of companies have broad-based stock option programs and that 37 per cent of them had broadened participation to more employees in the last two years (Lebow et al. 1999).

[5] This is based on a December 1993 Gallup survey and a January 1997 Princeton Survey Research Associates survey, summarized in Kruse & Blasi (1999).

plans for at least some employees.[6] The prevalence is higher among publicly held firms where profits are public information: close to two-fifths of public firms have profit sharing for employees (Kruse 1993, pp. 8–10). Most profit sharing is deferred, where the profit share is put into an employee retirement account, while about one-fifth of participants are in cash-only plans and another one-tenth are in cash or deferred plans where employees can elect whether to defer their profit share. Profit-sharing formulas vary widely among companies, with about one-third of companies having the share be fully discretionary from year to year (PSCA 1993; US BLS 1998).

We know less about other forms of shared capitalism. Gain-sharing plans typically tie employee compensation to a group-based operational measure—such as physical output, productivity, quality, safety, customer satisfaction, or costs—rather than to a financial measure such as profitability or returns. These plans often involve employees in some formal way to develop ideas and skills for improving performance. The three most popular types are Scanlon, Rucker, and ImproShare plans, although there is a growing number of custom-designed plans. About two-fifths (43 per cent) of Fortune 1000 surveys have gain-sharing plans somewhere in the company, although most include less than 20 per cent of employees (Lawler et al. 1998, p. 19). Broader surveys of compensation and human resource managers have found that only about one-eighth (13 per cent) have gain-sharing plans (Collins 1998). The percentage of employees covered is likely to be low since most firms with gain-sharing include only a minority of employees. All told, we estimate that about 25 per cent of the workforce has either a profit-sharing or a gain-sharing plan.

Adding together the proportion of workers with some ownership stake, profit or gain sharing, and with retirement funds invested substantially in company shares and taking account of likely overlaps among the groups, we estimate that on the order of half of the US workforce receives income that depends on the economic performance of their firm or work group.[7] We do not know, however, the depth of this dependence, i.e. the

---

[6] Calculated from data in US BLS (1999) and US Chamber of Commerce (1998).

[7] Employee ownership and profit sharing have also received substantial attention in other advanced countries and transition economies. With coverage similar to that in the United States, between 20 and 30 per cent of workers in France, Great Britain, Italy, and Japan are covered by some form of profit sharing, while smaller numbers are covered by employee stock ownership (del Boca, Kruse & Pendleton 1999; Jones & Kato 1993). Across the European Union, between 5 and 43 per cent of firms within each country have profit-sharing plans, between 1 and 22 per cent have employee share ownership, and between 5 and 38 per cent have team-based bonuses (European Foundation for the Improvement of Living and Working Conditions 1997). Employee ownership is also found in some socialist countries that are moving towards private ownership, including China (Tseo 1996), Russia (Blasi, Kroumova & Kruse 1997), and the countries in central and eastern Europe (Uvalic & Vaughan-Whitehead 1997; Smith, Cin & Vodopivec 1997).

proportion of income that depends on company or group performance for that half of the work force. This review clearly demonstrates that the development of employee equity programs (and shared capitalism programs in general) has now reached a level where it should rightfully command the interest of organizational behavior experts. The authors, together with Richard Freeman of Harvard University, have initiated the Shared Capitalism Project with a grant to the National Bureau of Economic Research from the Russel Sage Foundation and the Rockefeller Foundation to complete intensive case studies of representative organizations using these progams in preparation for a major national survey.

EMPIRICAL EVIDENCE: ORGANIZATIONAL BEHAVIOR ISSUES

We have recently reviewed all the empirical studies that we could identify that perform statistical analyses of data collected in a systematic fashion on employee ownership (Kruse & Blasi 1997; Kruse 1999a). These studies examine the links between firm performance, employment stability, firm survival, employee attitudes, and employee wealth and wages. These studies have looked at a variety of forms of employee equity. They have varied methodologically. Many make cross-sectional comparisons between firms with and without plans, some compare firms before and after the adoption of such plans, and some look within firms to measure the effects of different features.

Firm Performance

Over 32 studies in the past 20 years have examined the link between employee ownership and firm performance. The theoretical context for looking at the relationship between ownership organization and firm performance is examined in detail in a recent review by Kang & Sørensen (1999). The studies are split between neutral and positive findings. While the majority of studies could not firmly establish a link between employee ownership and performance, meta-analyses strongly point toward a positive link overall (there are far more positive results than would be expected if there is in fact no true relationship). Across both studies of employee ownership, the average estimated increase in productivity associated with these plans is about 4.5 per cent. Positive relationships do not, of course, establish causality. There may be selection bias in the firms that adopt these plans or workers who work under them. Good performance may be a cause, rather than an effect of employee ownership, or it may depend on other factors within the firm. The pre/post studies that control for the most basic form of selection bias find that productivity does increase on average following adoption. Studies that use various econometric shenanigans to adjust for the potential endogeneity of employee ownership find little substantive difference in the results. And studies on the types of workers who choose to work in employee ownership companies indicate that both high and low performers tend to avoid pay plans tied to group performance, and average worker quality is not very different under these plans, so that issues of worker quality are not likely to bias the firm-based estimates. A recent study (not included in this review) examined the relationship between broad-based stock option programs and firm performance and found substantial and statistically significant impacts on productivity and return on assets when the performance of the firms was compared with all public firms and with their industry group cohorts (Blasi et al. 2000; www.nceo.org/library/optionreport.html).

Employment Stability, Growth, and Firm Survival

Traditional analysis of labor-run firms predicts lower employment than in management-run firms, and perverse employment-reducing responses to positive demand shocks (reviewed in Bonin & Putterman 1987). Some scholars think that profit sharing, in contrast, may have positive effects on employment behavior (Weitzman 1984). Extant work suggests that the first prediction is erroneous, while the second is broadly correct. Employee ownership firms tend to have more stable employment rather than less stable employment than other firms (Craig & Pencavel 1992, 1993; Blair, Kruse & Blasi 2000). In addition, public firms with substantial employee ownership are more likely than other comparable firms to survive over time, while the stock market performance of the employee ownership firms is slightly better than that of other firms. Two studies have found that employment has grown faster in firms following the adoption of ESOPs, particularly if they have greater employee participation in decision-making (Quarrey & Rosen 1993; Winther & Marens 1997). The evidence therefore indicates that employee ownership may have significant potential for enhancing employment security, both through stabilizing firm employment levels and enhancing firm survival.

Employee Attitudes

Employee equity policies have the potential for improving employee attitudes and behaviors, particularly when used in combination with employee involvement and other complementary policies. Recent analysis of the Freeman/Rogers Workplace Representation and Participation Survey shows that while employee involvement has a larger impact on indicators of worker productivity, job satisfaction, and attitudes toward the firm than does financial participation, even higher outcomes occur when firms combine employee involvement, employee ownership, and pay linked to company/group performance (Freeman & Dube 2000; for a review of the entire national survey on the US workforce, see Freeman & Rogers 1999). There have been 29 prior studies on employee attitudes and behavior under employee ownership in the past two decades. The attitudes analyzed include employee satisfaction, organizational commitment or identification, employee motivation, and perceived and desired employee influence in decisions. The behaviors analyzed include turnover, absenteeism, grievances, tardiness, and injuries. An important result is that this research finds no automatic connection between employee ownership and either perceived or desired employee participation. The decision-making in a large number of employee ownership firms is no different than in conventional firms.

Overall, these studies find a non-negative relation between ownership and attitudes. Several studies find higher satisfaction, commitment, and motivation among employee-owners, but others find no significant differences between owners and non-owners, or before and after an employee buyout. Most studies find that organizational commitment and identification are higher under employee ownership, while giving mixed results between favorable and neutral on job satisfaction, motivation, and behavioral measures. Improvements in attitudes under employee ownership are almost always due to the status of being an employee-owner, rather than to the size of one's ownership stake. From our perspective, a key result in several studies is that attitudes and behavior are positively linked to greater perceived or actual participation in decisions rather than to ownership stake *per se*. However, these studies do not establish causality: better attitudes and behavior may lead to higher perceived or actual participation, or the two may reflect similar orientations to the company. The importance of participation finds support in the finding of Pendleton, Wilson & Wright (1998) that opportunities for participation in decision-making were more important than ownership *per se* in generating feelings of ownership. In sum, studies of employee attitudes and behavior under employee ownership tend to find positive or neutral effects of these plans. Several findings suggest better attitudes or behavior when these plans are accompanied by greater employee participation in decisions.

Employee Wealth and Wages

Do employees sacrifice other pay and benefits for a direct share in ownership, or do these simply add to worker income and wealth, and thus come out of increased productivity or economic rent that could have gone to shareholders? Workers in employee ownership plans do not in general have lower average wages or compensation than other workers. To the contrary, public companies with substantial employee ownership have 8 per cent higher average compensation levels than other comparable public companies, and average compensation increases with the percentage of stock held by employees (Blasi, Conte & Kruse 1996). A closer examination of pay and benefits in ESOP and non-ESOP firms found that ESOPs appear to add to worker rewards rather than to exist at the expense of regular pay and other benefits (Kardas, Scharf & Keogh 1998). ESOPs also appear to add to pension wealth, coming on top of other pension assets, but do not appear to affect the distribution of pay within firms. Similarly, employer stock held in 401(k) plans appears to come largely on top of other pension assets.[8] The available evidence thus finds little support for the proposition that workers are trading pay or other benefits for employee ownership. This may partly reflect higher average productivity levels in employee ownership (representing a compensating differential for greater expected effort) or the use of efficiency wages in combination with employee ownership to motivate workers. While one study indicates that ESOPs add to pension wealth, there has been no research on the important question of how employee ownership relates to the overall wealth of individuals.

Reasons for Adoption

Why do firms adopt employee equity programs? The 16 studies on this question do not support any one dominant explanation for the adoption of these plans (Kruse 1999a). Several show that firms are motivated by potential productivity gains. Others point toward a desire for greater flexibility in employee compensation. Some firms say they adopt or maintain such plans in part to discourage unionization by increasing company identification. In addition, some employee ownership plans were adopted to provide protection against hostile takeovers, although this was only a minor factor in the growth of employee ownership in public companies over the 1980s (Blasi & Kruse 1991). Tax advantages play a role in some countries, but currently in the United States—contrary to common belief among many social scientists who often do not understand the technical details of these tax incentives—there are almost no special tax incentives for employee ownership. ESOPs, 401(k)s, and deferred profit-sharing

---

[8] This result is from a Rutgers University Ph.D. dissertation by Kroumova (1999). 401(k) plans holding employer stock have substantially higher assets per employee, and are more likely to be in companies that also sponsor defined benefit pension plans, than 401(k) plans not holding employer stock.

plans have employee taxes deferred until the funds are received at retirement, but in this respect do not differ from other pension plans. This is a
very important and often missed detail. Many of the ESOP tax incentives
that existed in the 1980s have been terminated; the major remaining tax
incentives are that company owners can avoid capital gains taxes on
shares sold to an ESOP in private firms and leveraged ESOPs using loans
to buy shares can gain tax deductions for 25 per cent rather than 15 per
cent of taxable wages. In Japan, moreover, ESOPs have grown more
rapidly than in the United States without any tax advantages at all (Kato
1999). While an industry's competitive pressures may lead some firms to
adopt flexible pay plans, employee ownership tends to be distributed
broadly across industries (except that they are less common in the agri-
culture, mining, and construction industries). (For a detailed debunking
of frequent claims by social scientists that employee ownership is industry specific, see Blair, Kruse & Blasi 2000.)

WHAT DO WORKERS THINK?

Opinion polls have asked workers and the general public about their
attitudes toward employee ownership. We know from other surveys
that the majority have favorable views and value participation in company decisions highly (Freeman & Rogers 1999). But extant surveys
have not asked workers about the financial risks involved in ownership,
so they give a one-sided picture. Most workers express interest in
greater financial participation in their firms. A majority say they would
trade their next wage increase for a share in company ownership, and a
majority of young workers feel that employers 'fall short' in 'sharing
profits with employees', which is identified in a recent poll as one of the
four key areas in which young workers need help (AFL-CIO 1999). Most
members of the public think that workers in employee ownership firms
work harder and better, and are more likely to vote in the long-
term interest of the company. In a major 1975 poll two-thirds said
that they would prefer to work for an employee-owned and employee-
controlled company, as opposed to a company owned by outside investors or government. In another poll, more employees preferred an
ownership share to a pay increase, although even higher percentages
would prefer health insurance after retirement. A majority of the public
said that they would refuse to sell company stock to an outside investor
even for twice the market value of the stock. Only a minority, however,
prefer company-wide incentives to a straight wage salary. High-income
workers appear more willing to accept employee ownership and
company-wide incentives. But blue-collar workers were the most

interested in employee-owned and employee-controlled companies in the 1975 poll.

A majority of employees feel that they deserve more participation in company decisions, favoring organizations run jointly by employees and managers based on the view that managers must be deeply involved if worker participation is to be effective (Freeman & Rogers 1999). When asked to choose, a majority of workers say they would prefer participation to a greater share of ownership. At the same time, two-thirds in 1975 thought there had been too little discussion of employee ownership and control of companies. In a more recent 1992 poll, one-quarter said they know a great deal or a fair amount about employee-owned firms, one-third said they do not know much, and one-third said they know nothing. The generally favorable views of employee ownership indicate that it appears to touch upon some deep-seated notions about the value of ownership and the role of employees in the workplace. These results leave unanswered, however, questions about the depth of the support, or why people view these concepts favorably. Support for employee ownership may be based in part on the view that it provides more participation in company decisions (which is valued more highly than ownership by itself, when people are asked to choose). Similarly, support for employee ownership may be based in part on the idea that it provides extra job security (which has become more of a widespread concern in the 1990s) or more wealth (which appears to be the case).

CONCLUSION

It is clear that the division of organizational roles between owners who are founders, initial capitalist investors, managers, or outside shareholders in corporations *and* workers who simply get wages for hours has undergone a significant change in the United States. Workers are now owners and they are involved in management. A variety of forms of employee equity are becoming a significant minor phenomenon with a quarter of workers participating, and the overall format of modest shared capitalism approaches appears to be entering majoritarian status. A variety of sources suggest that multiple forms of employee equity are used in the same firm. Taking ESOPs and stock option firms alone, there are now thousands of US corporations where actual worker ownership is above 20 per cent or all broad-based employee stock options are above 20 per cent of total outstanding shares! If the 10 per cent cut-off point is used, then the number increases dramatically. Is capitalism somehow changing?

A simple perusal of organizational behavior journals, textbooks, case studies, and courses also reveals that these events have largely been bypassed by the field. Most of the empirical research is being done by economists, finance experts, compensation experts, or social scientists who are not in the organizational behavior tradition. Nevertheless, the really important questions about the employee equity phenomenon are particularly suited to the expertise and methods of organizational behavior specialists:

- Have employee equity programs created a new kind of corporation or are the programs ways to exert traditional hierarchical control?
- What characteristics determine that employee equity programs in a corporation have achieved some critical mass and have significantly changed traditional roles in that organization?
- To what extent does the success of employee equity programs depend on mere mathematical considerations, for example the per cent of ownership or fully diluted equity (in the case of broad-based stock option programs), the per cent of annual compensation in stock or stock options, the per cent of workers participating, and so forth?
- To what extent does the success of employee equity programs depend on the role that they play in a comprehensive program of strategic human resource management where they fit together sympathetically with other aspects of the high performance work organizations such as increased emphasis on selective recruitment, training, participation in decisions, access to information, performance evaluation, performance management, and so forth?
- Are economic considerations mainly driving the employee equity phenomenon, such as the tight labor markets, the cut-throat competition for professionals in high-tech, flat inflation-adjusted wages, the increased emphasis on performance in corporations, and so forth?
- Are changes in corporate culture mainly driving the employee equity phenomenon, such as democratizing tendencies in management, desires to reverse hierarchy, self-directed work teams, the growth of knowledge-dependent industries, and so forth?
- What are the key features of organizations that achieve significant increases in organizational commitment and/or financial performance from employee equity programs?

It is clear that the spread of employee equity programs has not taken place because of a strong emphasis on them by social scientists. Nevertheless, organizational behavior specialists now have an important role to play in helping the public understand how to manage this phenomenon.

Regarding the future, it is clear that the nature of firms is undergoing a gradual transformation occasioned by this increasing trend towards employee ownership. Indeed, the nature of firms themselves may be changed by the distribution of ownership, and entire assumptions about what firms are might change.

We now evaluate this transformation modestly as one happening in gradations from least transformative to most radical. First, the definition of the traditional firm is now open to question as workers own and manage. The role definitions of workers and managers and shareholders are collapsing. Academics, journalists, the public, and workers and managers themselves have not caught up with this. They are still pouring new wine into old wineskins! We cannot enumerate how many times we see a Chief Executive Officer (CEO) with more than 20 per cent employee ownership talk about her or his firm or read a reporter's story on such a firm or see an academic's case study of such a firm without any mention of worker ownership. If that is not the subject of the speech, article, or case study, it is often ignored!

Second, this reality is calling into question the power imbalance in firms from a very different perspective than the traditional perspective of labor versus management. What we mean is that worker-owners in the mainly non-union employee ownership sector in the United States largely have zero corporate governance rights (i.e. no independent non-senior managment board representation for their shares). As more and more workers, institutional investors, and policy-makers notice this inconguity, it will raise challenging questions. Most managers respond to this now by saying that they represent the workers, but obviously that is specious since most managers used to say that they represented all shareholders and thus needed no independent directors on their boards. That has all changed with the independent director movement in the Unites States. There will be an independent worker-director movement in the United States at the second stage of US corporate governance development and it will be dominated by non-union firms where workers have big equity stakes. This is how the European wind of German co-determination and the worker representation trend in EU countries will arrive in the United States in the next decade.

Third, widespread employee ownership will put additional pressure on how workers act inside firms. This will be in addition to the tough pressure now exerted on the traditional view of the corporation by the demise of hierarchical ideology in corporations, the rise of the knowledge worker and knowledge products, and the attitudes and habits and mores of the new workforce. Worker-owners will quickly recognize as the empirical evidence indicates that they can own 20 per cent of a firm and have little say over their work, work area, and work organization, and few levers to really make things better. If workers get a fixed wage for whatever they do short of bad behavior then they have little incentive to demand self-directed work teams. But that may be different if they are real partners in the firm (on this issue, see Rousseau & Shperling 2000).

REFERENCES

AFL-CIO (1999) *High Hopes, Litte Trust: A Study of Young Workers and Their Ups and Downs in the New Economy*. Washington, DC: AFL-CIO.

Blair, M., Kruse, D. and Blasi, J. (2000) Is employee ownership an unstable form? Or a stabilizing force? In T. Kochan & M. Blair (Eds), *The New Relationship: Human Capital in the American Corporation*. Washington, DC: The Brookings Institution.

Blasi, J. (1987) *Employee Ownership: Revolution or Ripoff?* New York: HarperCollins.

Blasi, J. & Kruse, D. (1991) *The New Owners: The Mass Emergence of Employee Ownership in Public Companies and What it Means to American Business*. New York: HarperBusiness.

Blasi, J., Conte, M. & Kruse, D. (1996) Employee ownership and corporate performance among public corporations. *Industrial and Labor Relations Review*, **50**(1): 60–79.

Blasi, J., Kroumova, M. & Kruse, D. (1997) *Kremlin Capitalism: Privatizing the Russian Economy*. Ithaca: Cornell University Press.

Blasi, J., Kruse, D., Sesil, J. & Kroumova, M. (2000) *Public Companies with Broad-based Stock Options: Corporate Performance*, Oakland, CA: National Center for Employee Ownership.

Blasi, J. & Kruse, D. (2001) *Employee Equity in the Internet 100*. New Brunswick, NJ: Rutgers University School of Management and Labor Relations.

Bonin, J. P. & Putterman, L. (1987) *Economics of Cooperation and the Labor-Managed Economy*. New York: Harwood Academic Publishers.

Bonin, J. P., Jones, D. & Putterman, L. (1993) Theoretical and empirical studies of producer cooperatives: will the twain ever meet? *Journal of Economic Literature*, **31**: 1290–1320.

Brickley, J. A. & Hevert, K. T. (1991) Direct employee stock ownership: an empirical investigation, *Financial Management*, **Summer**: pp. 70–84.

Collins, D. (1998) *Gainsharing and Power: Lessons from Six Scanlon Plans*. Ithaca and London: Cornell University Press, ILR Press.

Craig, B. & Pencavel, J. (1992) The behavior of worker cooperatives: the plywood companies of the Pacific Northwest. *American Economic Review*, **82**: 1083–1105.

Craig, B. & Pencavel, J. (1993) The objectives of worker cooperatives. *Journal of Comparative Economics*, **17**(2): 288–308.

Craig, B. & Pencavel, J. (1995) Participation and productivity: a comparison of worker cooperatives and conventional firms in the plywood industry. *Brookings Papers on Economic Activity*, 212–160.

Del Boca, A., Kruse, D. & Pendleton, A. (1999) Decentralisation of bargaining systems and financial participation: a comparative analysis of Italy, UK and the US. *Lavoro e Relazioni Industriali*, **Summer**.

Estrin, S. & Jones, D. C. (1992) The viability of employee-owned firms: evidence from France. *Industrial and Labor Relations Review*, **45**(2): 323–338.

European Foundation for the Improvement of Living and Working Conditions (1997) *New Forms of Work Organization: Can Europe Realize its Potential?* Luxembourg: Office for Official Publications of the European Communities.

Freeman, R. & Dube, A. (2000) Shared compensation systems and decision-making in the U.S. job market. Draft, Harvard University Department of Economics, and Centre for Economic Performance, London School of Economics

Freeman, R. & Rogers, J. (1999) *What Workers Want*. New York: Russell Sage and Cornell University Press.

Frohlich, N. & Oppenheimer, J. A. (1998) Employee versus conventionally-owned and controlled firms: an experimental analysis. *Managerial and Decision Economics*, **19**(4–5): 311–326.

Gates, J. R. (1998) *The Ownership Solution: Toward a Shared Capitalism for the 21st Century*. Reading, MA: Addison-Wesley.

Hansmann, H. (1996) *The Ownership of Enterprise*. Cambridge: Harvard University Press.

Investment Company Institute (1999) EBRI–ICI study shows workers favor equity funds for 401(k) plans. http://www.ici.org/about shareholders/ebri_ici_news.html.

Investor Responsibility Research Center (1998) *Potential Dilution at S&P Companies in 1998*. Washington, DC: IRRC.

Jones, D.C. (1979) U.S. producer cooperatives: the record to date. *Industrial Relations*, **8**: 343–356.

Jones, D. C. & Kato, T. (1993) Employee stock ownership plans and productivity in Japanese manufacturing firms. *British Journal of Industrial Relations*, **31**(3): 331–346.

Kang, D. L. & Sørenson, A. B. (1999) Ownership organization and firm performance. *Annual Review of Sociology*, **25**: 121–144.

Kardas, P., Scharf, A. L. & Keogh, J. (1998) Wealth and income consequences of employee ownership: a comparative study from Washington state. Draft, Washington State Department of Community, Trade, and Economic Development.

Kato, T. (1999) Report on changing participative programs in Japan. NBER, mimeo.

Keef, S. P. (1998) The causal association between employee share ownership and attitudes: a study based on the long framework. *British Journal of Industrial Relations*, **36**(1): 73–82.

Kruse, D. (1984) *Employee Ownership and Employee Attitudes: Two Case Studies*. Norwood, PA: Norwood Editions.

Kruse, D. (1993) *Profit Sharing Does It Make a Difference?* Kalamazoo, MI: W. E. Upjohn Institute.

Kruse, D. (1996) Why do firms adopt profit-sharing and employee ownership plans? *British Journal of Industrial Relations*, **December**.

Kruse, D. (1999a) Economic democracy or just another risk for workers: reviewing the evidence on employee ownership and profit sharing. Paper delivered at the Democracy, Participation, and Development conference, Columbia University, April. School of Management and Labor Relations, Rutgers University.

Kruse, D. (1999b) Public opinion polls on employee ownership and profit sharing. *Journal of Employee Ownership Law and Finance*, **11**(3): 3–25.

Kruse, D. (2000) The new employee/employer relationship. In D. Ellwood & K. Lynn-Dyson (eds), *Work and Future Society: What We Know, What We Value, What Should Be Done*. New York: Russell Sage Foundation.

Kruse, D. & Blasi, J. (1999) Employee ownership, employee attitudes, and firm performance: a review of the evidence. In D. Lewin, D. J. B. Mitchell & M. A. Zaidi (Eds), *The Human Resources Management Handbook, Part 1*. Greenwich, CT.: JAI Press.

Kroumova, M. (1999) Investment in employer stock through 401k plans: is there a reason for concern? Doctoral thesis. New Brunswick, NJ: Rutgers University School of Management and Labor Relations.

Kumbhakar, S. C. & Dunbar, A. (1993) The elusive ESOP–productivity link: evidence from U.S. firm-level data. *Journal of Public Economics*, **52**(2): 273–283.

Lawler, E., Mohrman, S. A. & Ledford Jr., G. E. (1998) *Strategies for High Performance Organizations*. San Francisco: Jossey-Bass.

Lebow, D., Sheiner, L., Slifman, L. & Starr-McCluer, M. (1999) *Recent Trends in Compensation Practices*. Washington, DC: U.S. Federal Reserve Board.

McNabb, R. & Whitfield, K. (1998) The impact of financial participation and employee involvement on financial performance. *Scottish Journal of Political Economy*, **45**(2): 171–187.

Mitchell, D. J. B., Lewin, D. & Lawler, E. E. (1990) Alternative pay systems, firm performance, and productivity. In A. S. Blinder (Ed.), *Paying for Productivity: A Look at the Evidence*. Washington, DC: Brookings Institution, pp. 15–94.

Nalobantian, H. R. & Schotter, A. (1997) Productivity under group incentives: an experimental study. *American Economic Review*, **87**(3): 314–341.

National Center for Employee Ownership (2000). *A Growing Number of U.S. Employees in Stock Option Plans*. Oakland, CA.: NCEO. Available at www.nceo.org.

National Industrial Conference Board (1928) *Employee Stock Purchase Plans in the United States*. New York: National Industrial Conference Board.

Ohkusa, Y. & Ohtake, F. (1997) The productivity effects of information sharing, profit sharing, and ESOPs. *Journal of the Japanese and International Economies*, **11**(3) 385–402.

Pendleton, A., Wilson, N. & Wright, M. (1998) The perception and effects of share ownership: empirical evidence from employee buy-outs. *British Journal of Industrial Relations*, **36**(1): 99–123.

Poutsma, E. (1999) *Financial Employee Participation in Europe*. Report to the European Foundation for the Improvement of Living and Working Conditions. Nijmegen, Netherlands: Nijmegen University Business School.

PSCA (1993) *36th Annual Survey of Profit Sharing and 401(k) Plans*. Chicago, IL: Profit Sharing Council of America.

Putterman, L. & Skillman, G. (1988) The incentive effects of monitoring under alternative compensation schemes. *International Journal of Industrial Organization*, pp. 109–119.

Quarrey, M. & Rosen, C. (1993) *Employee Ownership and Corporate Performance*. Oakland, CA: National Center for Employee Ownership.

Rousseau, D. M. & Shperling, Z. (2000) Pieces of the action: ownership and the changing employment relationship. Paper presented at the Academy of Management Meeting, Toronto, Canada, August.

Smith, S., Cin, B.-C. & Vodopivec, M. (1997) Privatization incidence, ownership forms, and firm performance: evidence from Slovenia. *Journal of Comparative Economics*, **25**(2): 158–179.

Tseo, G. (1996) Chinese economic restructuring: enterprise development through employee ownership. *Economic and Industrial Democracy*, **17**(2): 243–279.

Uchitelle, L. Economic view: stock option bonanzas vs. stagnant paychecks. *The New York Times*, **Sunday 21 November**: 4 (Business).

US BLS (1998) *Employee Benefits in Medium and Large Establishments, 1997*. Press Release USDL-99–02, Bureau of Labor Statistics, 7 January.

US Chamber of Commerce (1998) *Employee Benefits, 1997 Edition*. Washington, DC: US Chamber of Commerce.

US DOL (1999) Abstract of 1994 Form 5500 Annual Reports. *Private Pension Plan Bulletin*. Pension and Welfare Benefits Administration, U.S. Department of Labor, Number 7, Spring.

Uvalic, M. & Vaughan-Whitehead, D. (Eds) (1997) *Privatization Surprises in Transition Economies: Employee-ownership in Central and Eastern Europe*. Cheltenham, UK and Lyme, NH: Elgar, distributed by American International Distribution Corp., Williston, VT.

Webb, S. (1987). *Socialism in England*. London: Ashgate.

Weeden, R., Carberry, E. & Rodrick, S. (1998) *Current Practices in Stock Option Plan Design*. Oakland, CA: National Center for Employee Ownership.

Weitzman, M. L. (1984) *The Share Economy*. Cambridge, MA: Harvard University Press.

Winther, G. & Marens, R. (1997) Participatory democracy may go a long way: comparative growth performance of employee ownership firms in New York and Washington States. *Economic and Industrial Democracy*, **18**(3): 393–422.

CHAPTER 2

When Employers Share Ownership With Workers

Zipi Shperling
Tel Aviv University, Ramat-Aviv, Israel

and

Denise M. Rousseau
Carnegie Mellon University, Pittsburgh, USA

I'm looking forward to wheeling and dealing . . .—Miguel Cartagena, UPS driver, who became a shareowner when UPS went public after 92 years.

When the stock was going crazy it was difficult for employees to devote 100% of their attention to their jobs at hand—even though we have projects with starting at the stock price on computer screens and a lot of water-cooler conversations on when to cash out—Steven Ruben, VP Research, Human Genome Sciences.

Workers increasingly hold equity stakes in the firms that employ them. Firms worldwide have implemented equity sharing (e.g. stock option plans) for their employees (Schaefer 1996; Britain, *Sunday Times of London* 2000; New Zealand, Firth, Keef & Mear 1987; Blair, Kruse & Blasi 2000). Highly skilled workers increasingly are lured to start-ups promising them stock options with lower salaries than they can get elsewhere. As equity stakes are distributed among workers, managers, and financial investors, traditional differences in the meaning of capital/labor and owners/workers are being challenged (Rousseau & Shperling 2000).

This chapter addresses the motivations on the part of employers in offering equity stakes to workers. The 'employers' to whom we refer include the traditional owners of firms; that is, founders, financial

Trends in Organizational Behavior, Volume 8. Edited by C. L. Cooper and D. M. Rousseau.
© 2001 John Wiley & Sons, Ltd.

investors, and senior managers with significant ownership stakes. We address the impact of employer motivations on the nature of the ownership 'share' workers access, the co-occurrence of supporting practices that affect how effectively these motivations are fulfilled, and the research opportunities afforded by this change in the employment relationship.

THE MEANING OF OWNERSHIP

Ownership of a firm is a multidimensional phenomenon (Pierce, Rubenfeld & Morgan 1991; Rousseau & Shperling 2000). It includes financial participation, which entails access to profits and financial information, participation in decision-making, and a legal claim to the firm's assets should it be sold. Ownership also can encompass sociopsychological factors such as social standing, social responsibility, and psychological ownership (Rousseau & Shperling 2000). In the traditional employment relationship, the parties who have ownership (typically the firm's founders, financial investors, and managers holding stock) can view it as a source of power and influence. When a worker and an owner disagree over the rights and obligations each has (referred to as 'incomplete contracts,' Hart 1995), the owner has leverage. Disputes can more readily be settled on the owner's terms because of the owner/employer's control over the resources (e.g. equipment, materials) that make the worker productive and generate wages, the worker's major source of income. In the traditional firm, the owner can replace the worker more readily than the worker can find a new job.

The power associated with ownership is different in the modern firm than it has been historically. The value of a firm takes on different meaning as the mix of assets and resources that comprise firms change (Pfeffer 1994). What exactly do owners *own* in contemporary organizations? Traditional sources of economic value (thought of as forms of 'capital') include financial capital (i.e. access to cash or credit), capital equipment, intellectual capital (intellectual property embedded in patents and production processes), reputation or social capital (access to particular markets and clients based upon existing relationships), and scale economies. When a worker left the traditional firm, these assets remained under the control of owners. However, traditional assets need not afford the competitive advantage they once did. A combination of factors, including the expanded service sector, knowledge industry development, technological shifts, and globalization, has changed the mix of assets that give a firm its competitive advantage (cf. Reichheld 1994). The value of fixed assets, such as capital equipment, has declined precipitously in relation to the economic value inherent in the more variable assets composed of worker skills, the organization's ability to learn and adapt, and the strength of worker attachment to the firm (Pfeffer 1998; Leana & Rousseau 2000). As the economic potential residing in workers and their relations with the firm has become an increasing source of competitive advantage, the assets that traditional firm owners own have changed in both their tangibility and their controllability.

Our thesis is that if a firm's workers are not motivated to contribute to it, the firm is potentially far less valuable today than it would have been in the past. Expanding the allocation of ownership stakes to workers is a means by which entrepreneurs, senior managers, and financial investors seek to protect the value of their holdings. The attraction, motivation, and retention of skilled workers is increasingly characterized as a source of sustained competitive advantage (Pfeffer 1994). None the less, worker mobility—through both job loss and voluntary career moves—has become increasingly characteristic of employment in industrialized countries (Cappelli 1999; Jacoby 1999). The result is a shift in the power balance between firms and their highly mobile workers. (Note that less mobile workers can be disadvantaged under these conditions; see Carnoy et al. 1997; Rousseau 2000.) As one byproduct of this shift, firms are increasingly offering ownership to their workers, and employees are more often seeking equity stakes in the companies for which they work. Note that we use the terms equity, equity stakes, and ownership interchangeably in this chapter, using the standard definition of 'equity' as 'ownership interest possessed by shareholders in a corporation' (Downs & Goodman 1998).

There is a good deal of evidence that ownership is no longer just the domain of financial investors and senior executives. According to a statistical report of the National Center for Employee Ownership (November 2000), there are 11 500 ESOPS and stock bonus plans with a total assets value of more than US$400 billion, owned by 8.5 million participants. The growth of ESOPs was from 1600 plans in 1975 to 11 400 plans in 1998. In addition there are 4000 broad stock option plans with a value of several hundred billion dollars, owned by 8 to 10 million participants, and 4000 stock purchase plans, owned by 15.7 million (here is not realistic to estimate the value of plan assets). We can look back at 1990 and estimate roughly a million option holders and look at the present day and estimate roughly 7 to 10 million option holders. (National Center for Employee Ownership 2000). At the same time, American workers are increasingly identifying with their financial assets, not surprising since significant portions of those assets are in their employer's stock (Nadler 1998). Similar trends can be observed in the rest of the industrialized world. A quarter of the companies listed on the New Zealand Stock Exchange operated employee ownership schemes between 1976 and 1985 (Firth, Keef & Mear 1987). In Europe, a recent survey of entrepreneurial firms reported that more than 50% of responding firms had ESOPs, while another 25% planned to introduce such schemes in the near future (Thomson 1999). From these data, we conclude that equity stakes in firms are in creasingly shared between investors and workers. The focus of this chapter is on *why*.

DIFFERENT MOTIVATIONS TO SHARE OWNERSHIP

Why do companies grant ownership to their employees? We have begun a program of research examining the motivations of firm founders and senior managers for offering equity stakes to their employees. On the basis of our initial findings and a review of the business practice and organizational behavior literature, one conclusion is apparent: motivations for offering workers stock or stock options vary considerably among firms. Five major employer motivations appear to be salient (and employers act based upon one or more of these motives):

1. to recruit valued, often highly skilled, workers;
2. to retain them;
3. to motivate them to contribute highly to the firm, performing well individually as well as collectively;
4. to build a sense of community, enhancing worker identification with the firm; and
5. to respond to radical changes in economic circumstances.

Recruiting

Equity stakes, typically in the form of stock or stock options, are a device for attracting workers the firm might otherwise not be able to recruit. These tools are used in two distinct recruitment situations. First, under-capitalized start-up firms, particularly in high-technology areas, use the promise of an equity position in the firm to attract talent they cannot otherwise afford to pay (Taylor 2000). In this scenario the worker is motivated by the promise of a high pay-off in the future, in exchange for hard work and a lower salary today. Start-ups typically will give larger equity stakes to workers with higher market values.

While many traditional businesses were founded by people who intended to continue owning and operating them once they reached a level of profitability (Baron, Burton & Hannan 1996), high-technology start-ups are frequently developed to be sold so that their founders and investors can make sizeable profits (Taylor 2000). This shift in start-up strategy has happened at the same time that creating new businesses has gotten easier (e.g. due to less need for expensive fixed assets) and has accompanied a greater dependence upon knowledgeable workers who can be attracted by an equity stake. The promise of substantial wealth when a firm goes public (the widely publicized 'initial public offering') becomes the basis of what we term a 'blended' employment relationship, where workers are both employee and owner. Workers joining the start-up provide their labor in exchange for equity to be realized when the firm is sold, with their salary constituting a fraction of what they would otherwise earn. One perhaps unexpected twist of using equity stakes to attract highly mobile workers can be increased pressure to sell a relatively new business to outside investors before workers leave for other lucrative opportunities, including starting their own businesses.

A second reason stock options increasingly form part of a firm's recruiting strategy is pressure on established firms to compete with start-ups to hire qualified workers. Established firms find themselves needing to offer stock options to attract highly skilled workers who otherwise might find the promise of a windfall from start-ups enticing. As the proportion of start-ups offering equity to workers increases, such compensation practices become normative, changing the standards by which all potential employers are evaluated (Ingram & Simon 1995). Even established firms, including large Blue Chip companies from Disney to Xerox, find themselves compelled to offer stock options to would-be employees in order to compete with the promised wealth that start-ups offer (Parus 1998; Hansen 1999).

In both start-ups and established firms, employers may use the offering of equity not only as a recruiting strategy but as a form of 'golden handcuffs.' The retention of highly skilled workers can be facilitated by the use of a vesting period, wherein equity can only be accessed after a period of time with the firm. Firms benefit not only by retaining workers but by encouraging them to develop organization-specific skills and knowledge during this time period, increasing the likelihood that they will stay after vesting (Becker 1975).

Despite these similarities, start-ups and established firms do use stock options in significantly different ways. First, the economic value and psychological significance of equity stakes are likely to differ between the two types of companies. In an established firm, the expected value of the stock options, based on market factors, is often greater than in a start-up, because the firm is already publicly held and has a track record. Such firms are more likely to attract risk-averse workers. In contrast, the more risk-seeking may interpret the higher risk associated with start-ups as a psychological signal that the potential pay-off is significantly higher than in an established firm—a phenomenon observed in behavioral decision theory research, where high risk is associated with overestimation of the potential pay-off (Bazerman 1986). Selection effects can cause the risk-seeking and risk-adverse to sort themselves into start-ups and established firms. Such a selection mechanism can yield different sets of underlying motivations, different expectations regarding returns, and potentially distinct behavioral consequences as the recruit comes to face the reality of the firm's performance over time, or lack thereof (Taylor 2000).

A tendency to overestimate the possible pay-off from stock options in high-risk situations coincides with another non-rational aspect of potential worker reactions to stock options. Placement officers in MBA programs report that it is not uncommon for young MBAs to join start-ups based on the number of options they are offered while paying little attention to the overall size of the option pool (Eisel 2000). An MBA alumnus who chooses a firm offering 10 000 options over another offering 1000 may ignore the fact that the former offers less than 0.1 per cent of their total equity pool while the other offers 1 per cent of theirs. The promise of a high pay-off may lead recruits to overestimate its value, and ignore or downplay the risk of failure or the likelihood that their options will pay off.

The cost implications of stock options also differ for established and start-up firms. When start-ups and established firms compete to recruit the same workers, typically they are not offering employees the same compensation package (Heneman, Ledford & Gresham 2000). A low initial salary with the potential for a substantial windfall if the firm goes public and hits the jackpot (as in the frequently touted tales of millionaire Silicon Valley programmers and Microsoft secretaries) is the promise of the start-up. A market-based salary and good benefits coupled with a small but perhaps more reliable share of the profits is the financial package offered by an established firm (Heneman, Ledford & Gresham 2000). Each new hire in a start-up shrinks the potential pool of profits available to option holders in ways that are not really comparable for larger firms. The new hire in the established firm, however, costs the employer considerably more in the short run as higher salaries are paid along with stock offerings.

Implications

The above discussion of stock options in recruiting raises some questions. How does an employer's motivation to recruit using stock options affect the way ownership is distributed? What supporting practices co-occur to promote the use of stock options in recruiting?

In answer to the first question, we have made the case that the distribution of ownership is likely to be affected by the kind of firm doing the recruitment. It has become increasingly standard (i.e. normative) to use stock options as a device for recruiting highly skilled workers. But the purposes served by this device depend on the nature of the firm. These different purposes, in turn, influence the distribution of stock options across workers. Start-ups are more likely to vary the number of shares offered to workers, based on the criticality of that person's skills to the organization, since in effect, options are a substitute for direct compensation. However, this is less often the case in established firms, except perhaps in the case of top executives. Established firms are more motivated to offer options, not because they cannot pay workers a market-level salary, but because they compete for the same pool of skilled workers as start-ups, who offer options because they are unable to pay high salaries. Because they do not use equity stakes as a salary substitute in the same fashion as do start-ups, we would expect fewer differences between workers' equity positions in established firms than in start-ups. Established firms do have variations in ownership stakes based upon categories of workers (senior executives vs. middle managers vs. non-managerial workers), but we expect fewer differences within these categories. Wide disparities in compensation, which may be associated with perceptions of unfairness among workers, have been found to undermine firm performance and worker commitment (Cowherd & Levine 1992). How differences in ownership distributions affect issues of fairness and workforce commitment is an important topic for future research.

Our second question addresses the supporting practices that facilitate the effectiveness of equity as a recruiting tool. Stock and stock options are only part of a larger compensation package. Bloom & Milkovich (1996) argue that to understand the impact of compensation on worker and firm outcomes it is necessary to conceptualize it as a 'bundle' combining a variety of different compensation forms. There is a need for research on the behavioral and motivational impact of the compensation packages that bundle salaries with varying degrees of stock options. The relative proportions of pay at risk vs. guaranteed salary can signal different qualities in the employment relationship (Rousseau & Ho 2000). We know relatively little about how potential employees and new recruits interpret the mix of variable and fixed compensation and which combinations are more or less attractive to workers with different motives and values.

Equity stakes are becoming normative in many countries and many industrial sectors. One open question is how equity stakes affect worker attachment to the firm, whether they promote only continuance commitment or motivate deeper affective commitment (Meyer & Allen 1997). To date, the effects of workers having different equity positions within firms have not been investigated. Such practices raise questions regarding distributive justice within organizations and its effects on worker motivation and willingness to cooperate (cf. Taylor 2000).

Retention

It is increasingly apparent that workers who signal their marketability by obtaining outside offers and/or threatening to quit often can increase their compensation more quickly than colleagues who do not take such steps (cf. Berkovitch 1990). Research on selective rational exploitation indicates that employers are willing to pay workers they view as likely to quit more than workers seen as more likely to remain, even if the workers have the same skills and value to the firm (Lin, Insko & Rusbult 1991). Potential mobility gives workers greater power in the employment relationship, giving them leverage in negotiations with employers. The general trend toward worker mobility between firms has been implicated in the increasingly idiosyncratic psychological contracts that American and Canadian workers manifest (Rousseau 2000; Clark 1999) with more mobile workers better able to negotiate work arrangements reflecting their own personal interests and preferences.

Stock options coupled with vesting periods are used to retain mobile workers. The use of stock options as retention incentives has been encouraged by the British government (*The Sunday Times of London*, 27 February 2000), which proposes tax penalties for workers who withdraw their shares in less than five years. Not surprisingly, highly mobile workers are able to negotiate larger equity stakes and (paradoxically) shorter vesting times, especially when they first obtain offers from other employers.

Retaining people through the use of options with long vesting periods can be a means of promoting the development of organization-specific skills and knowledge (Becker 1975). Prolonged retention can add to an organization's competitive advantage, because organization-specific skills are difficult for competitors to imitate or acquire (Barney 1991). However, the risk of over-relying on vesting periods for retention is that other mechanisms that build worker commitment to the firm, such as trustworthy relations between workers and supervisors, procedural justice, and investment in worker development and career potential (Coff & Rousseau 2000), might be neglected in the process. We suggest that vesting periods alone might promote retention through continuance commitment, but will not necessarily enhance affective commitment without other practices in place that promote worker attachment to the firm.

The dilemma of rewarding self-interest while punishing loyalty is faced by those firms competing in tight labor markets. In its extreme, Frank & Cook (1995) describe the effects of the highly mobile upon their less mobile or more loyal counterparts as the 'winner takes all'. Workers who are less mobile and/or more loyal lose out as their salaries and equity stakes become lower and less equitable. Firms employing large numbers of highly mobile workers need to institutionalize such ownership arrangements, rather than face the equity issues associated with one-on-one idiosyncratic employment agreements (Rousseau & Shperling 2000). In such cases we would expect widespread offering of ownership rights to employees within firms with substantial proportions of highly mobile workers.

Implications

The use of equity positions to promote retention can lead to wide disparity in compensation between mobile workers and their less mobile counterparts. Firms run the risk of rewarding disloyalty and eroding the goodwill of loyal workers who do not threaten to quit. The behavioral and organizational consequences of rewarding workers differentially based upon mobility have received little attention in research on retention or in studies of distributive justice. We expect that firms largely composed of highly mobile workers will seek to institutionalize ownership arrangements with all workers to provide an attractive basis for retention while avoiding the dysfunctional consequences of perceived inequity and rewards for disloyalty (Adams 1965).

Vesting periods and other types of time-contingent compensation have received little attention in organizational research. Of particular interest are the means by which vesting periods give rise to more than mere continuance commitment among workers who remain with the firm to realize promised stock options. Research on the use of stock options to promote increased performance, which is reviewed below, suggests that bundling stock options with other benefits such as profit sharing may be necessary to induce higher worker contributions and attachment to the firm.

Enhancing Employee Contributions and Performance

Both new and established firms face the problem of how to motivate employees to maximize their efforts to contribute to firm performance. In the contemporary workplace, this classic problem is embellished by the marketplace's hyper-competition and the firm's heightened dependence on its workforce's skills and knowledge. The traditional formulation of this motivational challenge is the principal–agent problem, where the owner seeks to find ways effectively to motivate workers by using incentives to align worker interests with the owner's. Alchian & Demsetz (1972) suggest that pay cannot be based on an employee's direct contributions in terms of effort, intelligence, honesty, and imagination, since these cannot easily be measured. Hence, any effective financial incentive must be tied to individual results and/or organizational performance (Milgrom

& Roberts 1992). It should be noted, however, that agency theory proponents have traditionally considered employees to be too risk-averse to take on an ownership stake in the firm (Eisenhardt 1989). In contrast, the employment practices this chapter addresses suggest that not only is the general assumption regarding employee risk aversion questionable but so is the distinction between principals and agents as the boundaries between owners and workers blur.

Incentive pay based on individual or organizational outcomes can be useful for joining the actions of the agents with the firm's goals (Baker, Jensen & Murphy 1988; Jensen & Murphy 1990; Tosi & Gomez-Mejia 1989). Consistent with this concept, the use of incentive pay is positively related to total shareholder return and gross economic returns (Abowd 1990). On the basis of this notion, offering workers an ownership stake should increase their interest in the firm and its economic value to them (Milgrom & Roberts 1992). Hence, their greater contributions can result in improved firm performance.

Proponents of employee ownership have long assumed that it enhances firm performance (Tannenbaum 1983; Rosen & Klein 1983). Here we offer a brief review of the empirical literature. Rosen & Klein (1983) examined employment growth in 43 employee-owned companies and found that employment in these companies grew nearly three times as fast as in traditional firms. Similarly, Conte & Tannenbaum (1978) compared the profitability of 30 companies with employee-ownership arrangements. They found that companies with employee-ownership arrangements were 1.5 times more profitable than firms of comparable size lacking such arrangements. Wagner (1984) found that companies with at least 10 per cent employee share ownership performed equally as well on overall returns on investment as other companies in the same industry.

Yet, the research findings are not entirely consistent. Several studies have found that employee ownership had an adverse affect on profitability. Brooks, Henry & Livingstone (1982) found that ESOPs had no significant effect on profits. Similarly, in a survey of 100 companies with employee-ownership schemes, Tannenbaum, Cook & Lohmann (1984) found that profitability and financial growth did not differ from firms without such schemes. Even the data on employee attitudes are equivocal. While some studies find that satisfaction and reported motivation is enhanced by profit-sharing and share-ownership schemes (Bell & Hanson 1984, 1987; Fogarty & White 1988), others report no such improvement (e.g. Keef 1998).

Such inconsistencies, at the very least, suggest the existence of contextual differences that moderate the relationship of ownership, firm performance, and worker attitudes. Specifically, certain organizational characteristics can create difficulties in using equity stakes to motivate improved performance. Firm size and the relative impact of individuals on overall performance are examples of these difficulties. In large firms, the efforts of one individual may have little impact on the overall performance of the firm. Where improved stock price is the standard for evaluating performance, individual efforts can make little observable difference. Contrast this with professional service firms, which tend to be small, where individual efforts can make a visible difference (Gaynor & Gertler, 1995). Such firms often compensate their members through profit-sharing rather than methods based on changes in equity value.

In professional partnerships such as medical practices and law firms, the primary assets of the firm are its human capital and the reputation the firm has with its clients (Gaynor & Gertler 1995). Such firms have long blurred the boundary between owners and workers and between principals and agents. But even professional firms do hire employees who might not be owners. Since a partnership arrangement involves governance issues that limit its blanket use within a firm, other forms of employee ownership can also be used. Consider the accounting firm of Saltz, Shamis, and Goldfarb. To encourage staff to move toward partnership in the company, the firm leaders convinced 95 per cent of their senior-most CPAs to invest in the company by introducing an employee stock-ownership plan that has been highly successful. The idea behind the plan was to allow any CPA to purchase stock in the firm and participate in the economic benefits and challenges of ownership. It provided a fixed return and valuation-related return to the participants. Employees, as a group, engaged their own outside legal counsel to review the plan and brought the owners a list of questions, suggestions, and concerns. All their concerns were addressed. The firm growth rate in the year before the new partnership (1995) was 28 per cent. In the first six months of 1996, it grew at a rate in excess of 30 per cent, partner income increased by 20 per cent, and no voluntary turnover occurred (Shamis & Lewandowski 1996). The firm's plan returned 32 per cent to participants in the first year, brought in US$100 000 in employee investment, and provided the 120-person firm an important advantage in recruiting and retaining employees.

Coupling equity stakes with other practices associated with ownership can amplify the equity–performance relationship. Profit-sharing tied to firm performance and the use of other forms of incentive pay linked to worker productivity can be more effective in motivating performance than equity alone. Brown, Fakhfakh & Sessions (1999) observe that shared equity by itself reduced absenteeism by 14 per cent, while it reduced absence by an additional 11 per cent when coupled with profit-sharing. Profit-sharing alone reduced absence by 7 per cent. Ownership seems more powerful than profit-sharing in reducing absence, but best if introduced first and the other second.

It must be noted that profit-sharing only works where a firm has profits to share that can be realized in a relatively short term (e.g. quarterly or annually). Such profits are not always available, particularly in start-ups. Companies with more highly variable performance are most likely to implement both profit-sharing and employee stock-ownership plans since profit-sharing can be insufficient to motivate people in environments where profits are difficult to achieve (Kruse 1996).

Recent studies of publicly traded US firms indicate that firms using defined contribution pension plans investing in company stock and covering all regular workers had share returns averaging 6.9 percentage points higher over the four years after the ESOP was set up (Koretz 1999). These studies, like most others, do not take other aspects of ownership into consideration. We do not know whether these effects are independent of profit-sharing and other aspects of shared ownership such as high worker business literacy and shared financial information. Data do suggest that employee stock ownership is not sufficient to motivate sustained improvements in firm performance in and of itself. Bundling stock with profit-sharing and other individual or unit-level incentives is likely to provide a more effective motivator.

Profit-sharing also faces some limitations under higher levels of business risk. In turbulent environments, employees have been found to react negatively to incentive pay (Stroh et al. 1996). In a study of smaller firms engaging in initial public offerings, Beatty & Zajac (1994) reported that risk consideration influenced the use of incentive pay. High-risk firms engaging in initial public offerings tended to use stock options less frequently than did low-risk companies. In effect, as Bloom & Milkovich (1998) argue, higher business risk can undermine incentives even when employees are attempting to achieve the firm's objectives. It is perhaps for this reason that, after Microsoft's first wave of millionaires, co-founder Bill Gates mandated that newly wealthy workers cash out all but a portion of their Microsoft stock. By diversifying their financial holdings, Microsoft worker-millionaires would not have so much at risk that they could not continue to make the tough decisions that had made Microsoft successful in the first place.

High business risk makes it difficult for either principals or agents to determine what actions should be taken (Stiglitz 1987; Stroh et al. 1996; Bloom & Milkovich 1998). Greater business risk also makes it difficult to determine whether poor performance arises due to factors outside of managerial control or due to inferior managerial performance (Antle & Smith 1986; Milgrom & Roberts 1992). Difficulties in motivating and monitoring workers, which operate in all firms, are exacerbated in turbulent environments, such as are found in many high-technology firms.

Motivating performance through stock options is particularly complex in high-technology firms. The problems described above are heightened by the uncertainty regarding the firm's actual value or success. The ultimate evaluation of their efforts is often observed and evaluated by abstract entities ('the invisible hand' described by Chandler 1977) such as stock markets or potential (unnamed, unknown) buyers. Stock options are an attempt to motivate employees by rewarding outcomes that enhance the abstract and unknowable market value of a firm before the company goes public or is sold. Another factor, the high degree of interdependence among workers in high-tech firms, makes it more difficult to measure their individual contributions to the achievement of organizational goals (Simon 1991). From a broad perspective, the quality and success of a high-tech organization depends very little on the efforts of any single employee. The firm's value often is based on unique research and development processes that are difficult to measure or control.

Stock appreciation can occur due to market factors (i.e. a 'bull market'), even though a company's financial goals have not been met (Amazon.com and other e-business firms being a case in point). In addition, when an equity-based plan is 'globalized' (a common phenomenon in high-tech companies), the further complication of potential currency fluctuation must be considered as well. The value of a conventional option could be radically eroded or artificially inflated by changes in the relative values of currencies, totally apart from individual or corporate performance (Kroll 1999).

Implications

The data are not yet in on the link between employee equity ownership and firm performance. Moderator effects are likely. The nature of the firm, its size, and the financial and other organizational practices that are bundled with equity stakes are likely to play an important role in accounting for business performance. In high-risk environments, equity stakes may be more motivating when used in combination with profit-sharing. However, start-ups frequently have no profits to share. In such settings, individual and group-level performance feedback and other motivational supports may be necessary effectively to sustain motivation. Coherent combinations of ownership-related practices, such as profit-sharing, participation in decision-making, and feedback on financial status of the firm, reinforce a consistent message regarding organizational goals and values and the quality of the employment relationship. These practices also can provide motivational support through more frequent and interpretable performance feedback, which may not be available through stock price or option value alone.

To Build Community and Collective Identification

An important process that can occur throughout a person's life is 'identification,' the expansion of one's sense of self to include larger and larger sets of social entities (Coleman 1994). Identification brings with it expanded contributions from individuals who feel part of the larger collectives to which they identify. Monetary rewards may not in themselves foster identification; employment relations in which a monetary exchange is the primary focus often remain at arm's length, and largely economic in focus. There is a growing realization that an over-reliance on financial compensation gives rise to these transactional employee–employer arrangements, which competitors can easily copy or purchase. As Milkovich & Bloom (1998) note, 'Financial returns alone cannot extract the unique, value-adding ideas and behaviors possessed by employees. Financial returns alone are ineffective in creating the common mind-set that creates peoples' willingness to share the insights and tacit knowledge required to achieve and sustain advantage' (p. 22). However, when ownership entails a broad-based exchange, the worker is likely to identify with the firm.

Several ownership-related mechanisms foster identification. The first is the extent to which ownership is shared among organization members. Identification is likely to be lower where there is widespread inequity in the distribution of ownership (Rousseau 1998). A sense of 'we' is primed by common experiences, such as working together toward a common goal, and the downplaying of differences in status or benefits (Gaettner, Dovidio & Bachman 1996; Huo et al. 1996). If only the elite are owners, then identification can be undermined. On the other hand, when organizational membership offers individuals a broad spectrum of resources, including status, personal involvement, and concern for one's long-term well-being, employment can take on the significance of a personal relationship (Eisenberger et al. 1986)—even without an equity stake.

Incentive systems that attempt to align individual interests with organizational goals, such as stock options, are commonly used (Tosi, Katz & Gomez-Mejia 1997) but may have limited impact on perceptions of self in relation to the firm (Rousseau 1998). However, under certain conditions economic exchanges involving stock options or profit-sharing can signal a deeper relationship between the parties. Just as a Christmas bonus can be construed as a tribute to the employment relationship rather than just more pay, the ways in which ownership is shared affects workers' interpretations of it. For example, Intel paid US$820 million in profit-sharing in 1996, extending the principle of executive compensation to lower levels in the firm (Takahashi 1997). Intel sent a strong message of inclusion in its profit-sharing roll-out. In such circumstances, profit-sharing can go beyond paying people what they are worth on an external market, compensating them for contributions to firm profitability while signaling their connection to the firm's success.

Identification is likely to be fostered when shared ownership stakes are expanded to include profit-sharing, participation in decision-making, and access to financial information regarding the firm. We note, however, that in many firms where community building is not the motivation for equity-sharing, these latter practices are less likely to occur. None the less, accompanying equity-sharing with practices such as shared financial information can foster a sense of common fate, while participation in decision-making enhances the workers' sense of responsibility for organizational outcomes. The way firms treat people sends important messages regarding who people are in the eyes of a community (the firm as well as the worker's broader social environment). Treating workers as true owners gives them both status and power.

Integrating an organization's identity with an individual's self-concept as an owner has significant benefits for the organization (cf. Pratt 1998). First, identification can be integral to the commitment process. Weakened identification impedes worker trust and commitment, making workers less willing to contribute to organizational performance and lowering their psychological stability (e.g. Dutton, Dukerich & Harquail 1991; Buchanan 1974). In contrast, the employment relationship can be enhanced by creating a broader 'ownership identity' among employees. The creation of 'worker-owners' blurs the boundary between worker and firm, generating a moral commitment to work and organizational goals, and affecting employee attitudes and behaviors (Long 1981). Second, employees with equity stakes are often those with career opportunities outside the organization. The more that workers identify with the organization, the more they may recognize and develop opportunities in the internal labor market providing greater return on investments in human capital (Becker 1975). Third, identity is fundamentally a relational and comparative concept (Tajfel & Turner 1985). As internal and external signals focus on the differences between competing organizations, members can come to experience a greater sense of 'we', thus generating a greater willingness to cooperate with each other on the organization's behalf.

Expectations, shared information, and competence are important and interrelated factors that shape how workers respond to having an ownership stake in a firm. Equity holders' expectations regarding participation in the firm influence their actual participation and their satisfaction with the results (Pierce, Rubenfeld & Morgan 1991). It is not uncommon for ownership to be nominal, with workers continuing to think and act as workers rather than as participants with a greater stake in the firm. Rhodes & Steers (1981) report greater participative decision-making in worker cooperatives than is typical in conventionally owned firms, though conversion to employee ownership does not necessarily lead to greater worker control (e.g. Hammer & Stern 1980; Pierce, Rubenfeld & Morgan 1991). Also important is whether the management encourages worker-owner participation in decisions or shares relevant financial information with them (Hammer & Stern 1980). Participation is greater when financial information is shared with investors and workers (Berstein 1979). However, this sharing, particularly with regard to workers, is related to the level of business literacy they possess. Where workers possess little financial knowledge, typically they do not participate or are ineffective in their attempts to do so (Tannenbaum et al. 1974; Greenwood & Gonzales Santos 1992). Bundling ownership rights with financial information, participation in decision-making, and other supporting practices can enhance productivity by creating employment relationships based on high trust and spurring shared psychological contracts between employer and worker (Rousseau & Shperling 2000). This results in a distinct competitive advantage gained from a cumulative psychological engagement of workers with their employer.

Implications

Where building a community is the major goal of shared ownership, it is likely that stakes will be more evenly distributed across workers, since differential treatment can erode trust and the sense of 'we'. Shared ownership may have symbolic value that exceeds its financial implications. Research on community building in organizations suggests that trust and fairness contribute significantly to member identification and the formation of beliefs regarding community. Procedural justice is a major component of individuals' identification with their membership in larger groups (Tyler 2000). This form of justice relies heavily on the consistent or comparable treatment of group members, suggesting that equality in individual outcomes may be more valuable than differentiation. If community building is fostered by equality of outcomes, then it can be undermined by differential equity stakes based upon individual market value or status. Yet, how can equal outcomes and procedural fairness be reconciled with equity-based outcomes and distributive fairness? A dilemma can exist when employers desire to foster community while also attracting and retaining workers with particularly valuable skills.

Shifts in Ownership Structure due to Radical Change

Workers can become owners due to the forces of radical economic change. Two such radical changes are worker buyouts to salvage firms faced with closure and the allocation of ownership to the workers from the state or other controlling stakeholders due to political changes at the societal level (e.g. privatization) (Blasi & Kruse 1991). In both cases the academic and practitioner literature refers to these transformed organizations as cooperatives (e.g. Berman 1967; Berstein 1979).

Worker buyouts are typically motivated by the desire to 'buy one's job.' The announcement of a plant closing can cause workers to seek a way of avoiding job loss (Hammer & Stern 1980). Current owners of failing firms can salvage the financial value of their firms by offering them to motivated buyers—the workers themselves. Faced with job loss, workers have cashed in pensions or rolled pensions over into shares of the company for which they work. In many instances, state and local governments have provided financial assistance for the buyout. Because such buyouts are an attempt to save jobs, the investments are not made solely for the purpose of financial returns, and as a result they need not translate into perceptions of ownership (Hammer & Stern 1980). In effect, investment in a job does not equate to investment in a firm or give rise to psychological ownership. Research on worker buyouts indicates that workers continue to think of themselves as workers rather than owners and often display a preference for traditional managerial roles in decision-making, as opposed to decentralization. Location effects may play a role in the persistence of traditional thinking in these worker buyouts. Until the 1980s (at least according to the published evidence), most worker-owned firms were in rural areas with fewer alternative employers and lower workforce education levels (Stern & Hammer 1978).

Privatization of state assets is a second reason for shifting firm ownership to workers. In Britain, the privatization of local bus companies over recent years provides a number of examples of ESOP-type plans. One of the Britain's largest employee buyouts was that of West Midlands Travel (WMT) in 1990. The company's employee share-ownership scheme involved about 6000 WMT employees in a deal worth US$70.7 million. WMT was later sold to National Express for about US$244 million (Schaefer 1996).

The breakup of the Soviet Union has also led to privatization in many former Communist counties. Hungary, for example, has encouraged employee ownership of many former state-owned enterprises as a way to promote equitable economic development (Hungarian News Agency, 9 November 1998). In Eastern Europe, the privatization of formerly state-owned enterprises often has led to workers sharing ownership with banks (Goic 1999). Workers might hold onto their jobs, but profits accrue to the banks rather than workers, with little shift in the financial information or participation in decision-making away from traditional managerial roles.

Worker ownership arising from radical change often involves circumstances in which the assets have unclear or limited market value. Workers may have little inclination to act as owners in the making of financial decisions or in the sharing of risks, and they may expect few returns on their investments. However, the desire to have property rights in the midst of turbulence—to reduce the threat of job loss and unemployment—is probably the most important motivator from the workers' point of view.

Implications

The academic and popular literature refer to a variety of organizations as 'cooperatives'. However, the underlying dynamics of cooperatives differ greatly. These dynamics shape the human resource practices that differentiate cooperatives that have involved worker ownership from their inception from those whose ownership arises from radical and often difficult changes. Firms that were employee cooperatives from their inception, such as Mondragon (Greenwood & Gonzales Santos 1992), manifest more decentralized decision-making, more widely distributed financial information, and higher worker identification with the firm than is characteristic of either buyouts or privatized firms. Such cooperatives typically have elaborate human resource practices, beginning at the time of recruitment, which orient workers toward involvement in the firm beyond the traditionally narrow worker role. In these contrasting cases, worker expectations differ, as do their competencies regarding business issues.

Tannenbaum and his colleagues (Tannenbaum 1983; Tannenbaum et al 1974) have pointed out the importance of worker competence, particularly regarding business and financial issues, in shaping behavior where employees possess nominal ownership. Other factors include worker expectations regarding involvement in decisions traditionally made by the management. A key issue in both buyouts and privatized firms is the extent to which human resource practices emerge to help develop business literacy among workers and promote practices such as decision-making through worker councils.

NATIONAL CULTURE AND POLITICAL FACTORS

Looking to the future, it is fairly safe to say that worker ownership will increase in countries where it currently exists due to the employer motivations described above. However, firms in many countries face substantial barriers to the adoption of worker-ownership arrangements. Sharing ownership stakes in firms with workers is not legal in certain countries, and not culturally legitimate in many more. The long-standing social distance between workers and capital owners described by Karl Marx in the nineteenth century remains a social fact in many nations, supported by culturally ascribed roles. Governmental approaches to reducing labor–management conflict, as in the case of France and Germany, have reified the roles of owner and worker, making it culturally difficult for workers to think of themselves as owners even when firms are willing to take that step (e.g. Cadan 2000; Rousseau & Schalk 2000).

A European association of entrepreneurial firms, GrowthPlus, surveyed its member firms and found that although a majority had introduced ESOPs in recent years, they encountered both cultural and political obstacles. On the cultural front, the most important obstacles to stock-based remuneration were lack of employee familiarity with such schemes and low levels of business literacy among workers. Stock options were found to have a negative image due to their historical granting to senior managers, and a common perception that such plans are open to abuse (Thomson 1999).

Risk tolerance can also be shaped by national culture (Hofstede 1980; Rousseau & Schalk 2000). Workers may have little risk tolerance after prolonged exposure to 'sticky' wages that go up or stay the same but never decline (Lazear 1981), a particularly common feature of employment in continental Europe. Consider how Lufthansa implemented a successful ESOP among its largely German workforce (and note that Hofstede 1980 found that Germans scored relatively high on uncertainty avoidance, a form of risk-aversion). After facing worker resistance, Lufthansa added a twist to make the notion of stock ownership too good to refuse: employees could borrow money interest-free from the airline to buy additional stock at market prices. After two years, they could either sell the shares and pay back the loan or hold onto them and pay it off gradually. If Lufthansa's share price rose, then the employees pocketed the profit; if it sank, then the company promised to buy back the shares at no loss to the employee (Tagliabue 1998). The role of risk tolerance, and the presence of societal supports that make risk acceptable or not (e.g. pension security), are important issues for future research on expanded worker ownership. A blended employment relationship where workers are also at least partial owners of the firm can require cultural and institutional adjustments.

Political obstacles to worker equity stakes also vary widely from country to country. In some nations, stock markets have no legal or fiscal frameworks for dealing with ESOPs. In others, tax laws discourage the use of options. The benign tax environment in the United States has promoted the use of share options. Although increasingly seen as a competitive advantage, particularly by European firms, Europe-wide harmonization of taxation practices may be necessary for stock options to become an effective instrument to boost job creation and performance gains (Thomson 1999).

In summary, worker ownership is an innovation that can offer firms a competitive advantage; societies that do not today support such practices are likely to find themselves under pressure to adapt their political and cultural institutions to help their local firms compete globally.

CONCLUSION

As Tannenbaum (1983) commented many years ago, 'ownership is complicated.' The trend toward equity ownership confounds the roles of labor and capital because it means that both financial investors and workers are more and more often finding themselves sharing ownership. From the perspective of organizational behavior and theory, this trend suggests a fundamental shift in many of our traditional notions regarding firm performance, incentives, and the roles of owners, managers, and workers. It also raises intriguing questions regarding how equity stakes motivate workers and under what conditions the goals that motivate employers to share equity with workers can be realized.

Our assessment of existing research suggests two things. First, equity stakes might need to be bundled with other practices to produce higher worker performance, commitment, and retention. Unfortunately, research typically fails to consider the broader array of human resource and compensation practices with which stock and some options are bundled. Second, the ways in which the ownership pie is divided to achieve a particular employer motivation, such as attracting highly qualified workers, may conflict with the means to accomplish other employer motivations such as community building. Because the same employer can have several motives for sharing equity stakes with workers, the decision regarding their allocation is even more complicated than previously recognized.

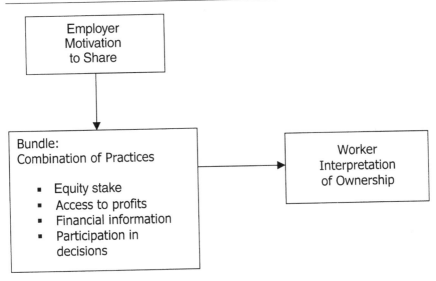

Figure 2.1 Bundling ownership practices

ACKNOWLEDGEMENTS

We thank Jason Merante for his research assistance in preparing this chapter and Paul Goodman and Wolfgang Weber for their comments. We also thank Catherine Senderling for her usual superb editing.

REFERENCES

Abowd, J.M. (1990) Does performance-based managerial compensation affect corporate performance? *Industrial and Labor Relations Review*, **43**: 52S–73S.

Adams, J. S. (1965) Inequity in social exchange. In L. Berkowitz (Ed.), *Advances in Experimental Social Psychology*, **2**: 267–299.

Alchian, A. & Demsetz, H. (1972) Production, information costs, and economic organization. *Quarterly Journal of Economics*, **90**: 599–617.

Antle, R. & Smith, A. (1986) An empirical investigation of the relative performance evaluation of corporate executives. *Journal of Accounting Research*, **24**: 1–39.

Arthur, M. B., Inkson, K. & Pringle, J. K. (1999) *The New Careers: Individual Action and Economic Change*. London: Sage.

Baker, G. P., Jensen, M. C. & Murphy, K. J. (1988) Compensation and incentives: practice versus theory. *Journal of Finance*, **33**: 593–616.

Barney, J. B. (1991) Firm resources and sustained competitive advantage. *Journal of Management*, **17**: 99–120.

Baron, J. N., Burton, M. D. & Hannan, M. T. (1996) The road taken: origins and evolution of employment systems in emerging companies. *Industrial and Corporate Change*, **5**: 239–275.

Bazerman, M. (1986) *Managerial Decision Making*. New York: Wiley.

Beatty, R. P. & Zajac, E. J. (1994) Managerial incentives, monitoring, and risk bearing: a study of executive compensation, ownership and board structure in initial public offerings. *Administrative Science Quarterly*, **39**: 313–335.

Becker, G. S. (1975) *Human Capital and the Personal Distribution of Income: An Analytical Approach*. National Bureau of Economic Research, New York: Columbia University Press.

Berman, K. V. (1967) *Worker-owned Plywood Companies: An Economic Analysis*. Pullman: Washington State University Press.

Berkovitch, E. (1990) A stigma theory of unemployment duration. In Y. Weiss & G. Fishelson (Eds), *Advances in the Theory and Measurement of Unemployment*. Hong Kong: Macmillan, pp. 20–56.

Berstein, P. (1979) *Workplace Democratization: Its Internal Dynamics*. New Brunswick, NJ: Transaction Books.

Blair, M., Kruse, D. & Blasi, J. (2000) Is employee ownership an unstable form? Or a stabilizing force? In T. Kochan & M. Blair, (Eds), *The New Relationship Capital in the American Corporations*. Washington, DC: Brookings Institution Press.

Blasi, J. & Kruse, D. (1991) *The New Owners: The Mass Emergence of Employee Ownership, Public Companies and What it Means to American Business*. New York: Harper Business.

Bloom, M. C. & Milkovich, G. T. (1996) Issues in managerial compensation. In C. L. Cooper and D. M. Rousseau (Eds), *Trends in Organizational Behavior*, Vol. 3, Chichester: Wiley, pp. 23–47.

Bloom, M. & Milkovich, G.T. (1998) Relationship among risk, incentive pay, and organizational performance. *Academy of Management Journal*, **41**(3): 283–297.

Brooks, L., Henry, J. & Livingstone, D. (1982) How profitable are employee stock ownership plans? *Financial Executive*, **May**.

Brown, S., Fakhfakh, F. & Sessions, J. (1999) Absenteeism and employee profit sharing: an empirical analysis based on French panel data, 1981–1991. *Industrial and Labor Relations Review*, **52**: 234–251.

Buchanan, B. (1974) Building organizational commitment: the socialization of managers in work organizations. *Administrative Science Quarterly*, **19**: 533–546.

Cadan, L. (2000) Does psychological contract theory work in France? In D. M. Rousseau & R. Schalk (Eds), *Psychological Contracts in Employment: Cross-national Perspectives*. Newbury Park, CA: Sage.

Cappelli, P. (1999) Career jobs are dead. *California Management Review*, **42**: 146–167.

Carnoy, M., Castells, M. & Benner C. (1997) Labor markets and employment practices in the age of flexibility: A case study of Silicon Valley. *International Labor Review*, **136**(1): 27–48.

Chandler, A. D. (1977) *The Visible Hand: The Managerial Revolution in American Business*. Cambridge, MA: Harvard Business School Press.

Clark, V. S. (1999) Making sense of part-time professional work arrangements. Doctoral dissertation, University of British Columbia, Vancouver, BC, Canada.

Coff, R. & Rousseau, D. M. (2000) Sustainable competitive advantage from relational wealth. In C. R. Leana & D. M. Rousseau (Eds), *Relational Wealth: The Advantages of Stability in a Changing Economy*. New York: Oxford University Press.

Coleman, J. S. (1994) *Foundations of Social Theory*. Cambridge, MA: Harvard University Press

Conte, M. & Tannenbaum, A. S. (1978) Employee-owned companies: Is the difference measurable? *Monthly Labor Review*, **101**: 23–28.

Cowherd, D. M. & Levine, D. I. (1992) Product quality and pay equity between lower-level employees and top management: an investigation of distributive justice theory. *Administrative Science Quarterly,* **37**: 302–320.

Downs, J. & Goodman, J. E. (1998) *Dictionary of Finance and Investment Terms,* 5th edn. Haupphage, NY: Barrons.

Dutton, J. E., Dukerich, J. M. & Harquail, C. V. (1994) Organizational images and member identification. *Administrative Science Quarterly,* **39**: 239–263.

Eisel, J. (2000) Personal communication, March, Carnegie Mellon University, Pittsburgh, PA.

Eisenberger, R., Huntington, R., Hutchinson, S. & Sowa, D. (1986) Perceived organizational support. *Journal of Applied Psychology,* **71**: 271–290.

Eisenhardt, K. M. (1989) Agency theory: an assessment and review. *Academy of Management Review,* **14**: 57–74.

Firth, M., Keef, S. & Mear, R. (1987) Some preliminary evidence on employee share ownership schemes in New Zealand listed companies. *New Zealand Journal of Industrial Relations,* **12**: 23–30.

Frank, R. & Cook, P. (1995) *The Winner-Take-All Society.* New York: Free Press.

Fogarty, M. & White, M. (1988) *Share Schemes as Workers See Them.* London: Policy Studies Institute.

Gaynor, M. & Gertler, P. (1995) Moral hazard and risk spreading in partnerships. *RAND Journal of Economics,* **26**: 591–613.

Gaettner, S. L., Dovidio, J. F. & Bachman, B. A. (1996) Revisiting the contact hypothesis: The induction of a common group identity. *International Journal of Intercultural Relations,* **20**: 271–290.

Goic, S. (1999) Employees' attitudes toward employee ownership and financial participation in Croatia: experiences and cases. *Journal of Business Ethics,* **21**: 145–155.

Greenwood, D. & Gonzales Santos, J.L. (1992) *Industrial Democracy as Process: Participatory Action Research in the Fagor Cooperative Group of Mondragon.* Stockholm: Arbetslivscentrum.

Hammer, T. H. & Stern, R. M. (1980) Employee ownership: implications for the organizational distribution of power. *Academy of Management Journal,* **23**: 78–100.

Hansen, E. L. (1999) More companies give stock options to broad number of employees. *ACA News,* **12 September**.

Hart, O. (1995) *Firms, Contracts, and Financial Structure.* Oxford: Clarendon Press.

Heneman, R. L., Ledford, G. E. & Gresham, M. T. (2000) The changing nature of work and its effects on compensation design and delivery. In S. L. Rynes & B. Gerhart (Eds), *Compensation in Organizations: Current Research and Practice.* San Francisco: Jossey-Bass, pp. 195–240.

Hofstede, G. (1980) *Culture's Consequences: International Differences in Work-related Values.* Newbury Park, CA: Sage.

Huo, Y. J., Smith, H. J., Tyler, T. R. & Lind, E. A. (1996) Superordinate identification, subgroup identification, and justice concerns: is separatism the problem? Is assimilation the answer? *Psychological Science,* **7**: 40–45.

Ingram, P. & Simon, T. (1995) Disentangling resource dependence and institutional explanations of organizational practice: the case of organizations' adoption of flextime and work at home. *Academy of Management Journal,* **38**: 1466–1482.

Jacoby, S. M. (1999) Are career jobs headed for extinction? *California Management Review,* **42**: 123–145.

Jensen, M. C. & Murphy, K. J. (1990) Performance pay and top-management incentives. *Journal of Political Economy,* **98**: 225–264.

Keef, S. P (1998) The causal association between employee share ownership and attitudes: a study based on the Long framework. *British Journal of Industrial Relations*, **36**: 73–82.

Koretz, G. (1999) ESOP benefits are no fables. *Business Week*, **6 September**: 26.

Kroll, A. H. (1999) Equity compensation in the global marketplace. *Human Resource Focus*, **August**: 4–8.

Kruse, D. L. (1996) Why do firms adopt profit-sharing and employee ownership plans? *British Journal of Labor Relations*, **43**: 515–538.

Lazear, E. P. (1981) Agency earnings profiles, productivity, and hours restrictions. *American Economic Review*, **71**: 606–620.

Leana, C. R. & Rousseau, D. M. (2000) *Relational Wealth: The Advantages of Stability in a Changing Economy*. New York: Oxford University Press.

Lin, Y. W., Insko, C. A. & Rusbult, C.L. (1991) Rational selective exploitation among Americans and Chinese: General similarity, with one surprise. *Journal of Applied Social Psychology*, **21**: 1169–1206.

Lind, E. A., Tyler, T. R. & Huo, Y. J. (1997) Procedural context and culture: Variation in the antecedents of procedural justice judgments. *Journal of Personality and Social Psychology*, **73**: 767–780.

Long, R. J. (1981) The effects of formal employee participation in ownership and decision making on perceived and desired patterns of organizational influence: A longitudinal study. *Human Relations*, **31**(10): 847–877.

MIT Hungarian News Agency (1998) 200 companies still under ESOP ownership. On line. Available http://www.Lexis-Nexis.com/universe.

Meyer, J. P. & Allen, N. J. (1997) *Commitment in the Workplace*. Thousands Oaks, CA: Sage.

Milkovich, G. T. & Bloom, M. (1998) Rethinking international compensation. *Compensation and Benefits Review*, **30**(1): 15–23

Milgrom, P. & Roberts, J. (1992) *Economics, Organization and Management*. Englewood Cliffs, NJ: Prentice-Hall.

Nadler, R. (1998) Stocks populi: as workers join the investing class, America may undergo a political realignment. *National Review*, **9 March**: 36–39

National Center for Employee Ownership (NCEO) (2000) A brief introduction to employee ownership. (Internet: http://www.nceo.org/library/eo–basics.html).

Parus, B. (1998) Stock becoming prevalent as compensation tool. *ACA News*, **September**: 12–15.

Pfeffer, J. (1994) *Competitive Advantage Through People: Problems and Prospects for Change*. Boston, MA: Harvard Business School Press.

Pfeffer, J. (1998) *The Human Equation*. Boston, MA: Harvard Business School Press.

Pierce, J. L., Rubenfeld, S. A. & Morgan, S. (1991) Employee ownership: a conceptual model of process and effects. *Academy of Management Review*, **16**: 121–144.

Pratt, M. G. (1998) To be or not to be? Central questions in Organizational identification. In D. A. Whetten & P. C. Godfrey (Eds), *Identity in Organizations*. Thousand Oaks, CA.: Sage.

Reichheld, F. F. (1996) *Loyalty Effect: The Hidden Force Behind Growth, Profits and Lasting Value*. Boston, MA: Harvard Business School Press.

Rhodes, S. R. & Steers, R. M. (1981) Conventional versus worker-owned organizations. *Human Relations*, **34**: 1013–1035.

Rosen, C. & Klein, K. J. (1983) Job creating performance of employee-owned firms. *Monthly Labor Review*, **106**(8): 15–19.

Rousseau, D. M. (1998) Why workers still identify with organizations. *Journal of Organizational Behavior*, **19**: 217–33.

Rousseau, D. M. (2000) Psychological contracts in the United States: diversity, individualism, and associability. In D. M. Rousseau & R. Schalk (Eds), *Psycho-*

logical Contracts in Employment: Cross-National Perspectives. Newbury Park, CA: Sage.

Rousseau, D. M. & Ho, V. T. (2000) Psychological contract issues in compensation. In S. L. Rynes & B. Gerhart (Eds), *Compensation in Organizations: Current Research and Practice*. San Francisco: Jossey-Bass, pp. 273–310.

Rousseau, D. M. & Schalk, R. (Eds) (2000) *Psychological Contracts in Employment: Cross-National Perspectives*. Newbury Park, CA: Sage.

Rousseau, D. M. & Shperling, Z. (2000) Pieces of the action: ownership, power and the psychological contract. Paper presented at the Academy of Management meetings, August, Toronto.

Schaefer, E. (1996) The development of ESOP in Europe. *European Venture Capital Journal*, **1 July**.

Shamis, G. S. & Lewandowski, N. (1996) A piece of the action: When one firm offered its professionals a chance to become owners, everyone benefited. *Journal of Accountancy*, **182**: 52–55.

Simon, H. A. (1991) Organizations and markets. *Journal of Economic Perspectives*, **5**: 25–44.

Stern, R. J. & Hammer, T. H. (1978) Buying your job: factors affecting the success or failure of employee acquisition attempts. *Human Relations*, **31**: 1101–1117.

Stiglitz, J. E. (1987) The design of labor contracts: the economics of incentives and risk-sharing. In H. R. Nalbantian (Ed.), *Incentives, Cooperation and Risk Sharing*. Totowa, NJ: Rowan & Littlefield, pp. 47–68.

Stroh, L., Brett, J. M., Bauman, J. P. & Reilly, A. H. (1996) Agency theory and variable compensation strategies. *Academy of Management Journal*, **39**: 751–767.

Sunday Times of London (2000) Labour unveils new incentives for workers. *Sunday Times of London*, **27 February**.

Tagliabue, J. (1998) Picking economic universe in Europe and Asia: in the old world a new equity culture. *International Herald Tribune*, **March**.

Tajfel, H. & Turner, J.C. (1985) The social identity theory of intergroup behavior. In S. Worchel & W. G. Austin (Eds), *The Psychology of Intergroup Relations*, Vol. 2. Thousand Oaks, CA: Sage, pp. 7–24.

Takahashi, D. (1997) Hey, big spender: Intel shares wealth with its employees – chip colossus paid $820 million in profit sharing in 1996; Options to be offered to all. *Wall Street Journal*. New York: February 12.

Tannenbaum, A. S. (1983) Employee-owned companies. In B. M. Staw & L. L. Cummings (Eds), *Research in Organizational Behavior*, Vol. 15. Greenwich, CT: JAI Press, pp. 235–268.

Tannenbaum, A. S., Cook, H. & Lohmann, J. (1984) *The relationship of Employee Ownership to the Technical Adaptiveness and Performance of Companies*. Ann Arbor, MI: Institute for Social Research, University of Michigan.

Tannenbaum, A. S., Kavcic, B., Rosner, M., Vianello, M. & Wieser, G. (1974) *Hierarchy in Organizations: An International Comparison*. San Francisco: Jossey-Bass.

Taylor, C. (2000) Is this the end.com? *Time*, **2 July**: 42–45.

Thomson, A. (1999) Growth companies press for share options reform. *European Venture Capital Journal*, **October**.

Tosi, H. L. & Gomez-Mejia, L. R. (1989) The decoupling of CEO pay and performance: An agency theory perspective. *Administrative Science Quarterly*, **34**: 169–189.

Tosi, H. L., Katz, J. P. & Gomez-Mejia, L. R. (1997). Disaggregating the agency contract: the effects of monitoring, incentive alignment, and terms in office on agent decision making. *Academy of Management Journal*, **40**: 82–111.

Tyler (2000) Social justice: Outcome and procedure. *International Journal of Psychology*, **35**: 117–125.

Wagner, I. (1984) Report to the New York Exchange on the performance of publicly held employee ownership companies. Unpublished Manuscript, Arlington, VA: National Center for Employee Ownership.

CHAPTER 3

The Psychological Consequences of Employee Ownership: on the Role of Risk, Reward, Identity and Personality

Paul R. Sparrow
University of Sheffield, UK

STOCK OWNERSHIP, RISK AND THE COMPENSATION LOTTERY?

Employee ownership, like many other trends in human resource management (HRM) such as virtual working or internationalization, is a phenomenon that comes in many different variations, and to many different degrees. It can range from full-shared ownership of a venture, through significant levels of involvement in the running of a venture, to financial participation (to varying degrees of total ownership levels or employee total remuneration package), and finally to more token 'stakes' and shared risks in the financial performance of the firm. As we work up this scale of engagement with the ownership process, we find fewer examples. We also find very different psychological consequences. This chapter focuses on some of the more recent initiatives and debates, using stock ownership as the main vehicle for discussion. This is something that *might* herald fairly dramatic changes in organizational behaviour, or might have a rather soft or localized influence on behaviour, depending very much on the extent to which employee ownership permeates the

Trends in Organizational Behavior, Volume 8. Edited by C. L. Cooper and D. M. Rousseau.
© 2001 John Wiley & Sons, Ltd.

workforce, and the degree of ownership that is granted. This chapter will raise a number of themes associated with employee ownership and consider some of the implications for organization behaviour research. The themes are of course inter-linked: risk; reward; identity, and personality.

The theme of shared risk is appropriate, because, excepting initiatives such as dot.com start-up situations where employee ownership might be motivated by the need to generate venture capital, in the main it is a concept pursued by larger more established organizations in an attempt to improve motivation, commitment, and involvement, and to deal with issues of fairness and equity in reward. To understand this trend, it is necessary first to understand the rewards strategy of organizations in the 1990s. Certainly in the United Kingdom there was a discernible trend pursued by the majority of organizations. It became known as the 'new pay formula' (Sparrow 2000b). Organizations found themselves operating in highly uncertain and very volatile markets. The major costs associated with employees were fixed, indeed rising, and not linked to the economic upturns or downturns of the business. The only way of controlling pay costs was to gain more control and autonomy at the organizational level and to make them more variable, by increasing the 'at risk' and variable elements. This was initially achieved through such things as individual performance-related pay, group bonuses, and company-wide profit-related schemes. In order to do this, organizations needed to minimize external regulation from governments, pan-national institutions, and trade unions. They also needed to introduce more flexibility into the internal HRM systems, and so this risk-sharing approach to reward was accompanied by parallel developments in broad-banding in order to increase managerial discretion over pay levels and enable a closer match with market pay rates. A process of individualization in rewards and benefits was also taking place, through cafeteria benefits and performance-related pay. The concern that many organizations had was that their rewards systems were proving to be dysfunctional, and certainly were not producing the desired outcomes. In short, organizations were reducing the long-term fixed costs associated with employment, moving to more immediate and direct forms of reward, and creating a shared risk performance culture (Sparrow 2000b).

Employee ownership, for many organizations, is proving to be the next step. In profit-related pay schemes employees are rewarded for their contribution to the business by linking a proportion of their reward to actual profits. The motivation of organizations here is to provide greater flexibility in the negotiation of pay and to improve motivation and commitment. In the United Kingdom for example, there are 7000 live schemes covering some two million employees (Gennard & Judge 1999). Share ownership takes financial involvement and participation a step further by giving employees a stake in, and involvement in, the ownership of the enterprise (indirectly) through voting rights. It also engenders (in theory) a longer-term commitment beyond the immediate financial gains of shared profits.

The proportion of employees who work in small and medium-sized enterprises—or family owned enterprises—is actually quite high in a number of countries. In this sense in several countries employees have developed psychological contracts in a setting that is close to the economic process, and more risky than the (now rapidly vanishing) traditional employment relationship was deemed to be. Indeed, there has long been a tradition for profit-sharing schemes in France (especially amongst the cadre), and for financial participation schemes in medium-sized owner-managed companies in Germany (Beardwell & Holden 1997).

To many outside the United States the current explosion of employee ownership through stock options is however seen as a very high-risk strategy, a compensation lottery. Perhaps this is because in the United States there is a strong ideal of ownership amongst an enterprise culture, stronger certainly than many parts of Europe, despite some openness to financial participation. Yet, the US situation has proved fascinating. Consider the following business press analyses. A recent conservative estimate by the National Centre for Employee Ownership (www.nceo.org) stated that between seven and ten million US employees participate in some sort of stock ownership program (Mahoney 2000). Stock options were initially offered in the 1960s to CEOs to boost personal income and shareholder value. Huge windfalls were made in the 1980s as stock markets boomed and tax rates were lowered. However, the device has spread into compensation packages for more and more employees. The total value of shares set aside for option grants in the US rose from US$59 to US$600 billion from 1985 to 1996 and more than 90 per cent of public companies now have employee ownership programmes (Greengard 1999). Stock options are becoming a preferred element of compensation packages and are no longer strange devices to employees, who are more in touch with markets and who act as consumers. They have become a popular way to attract and retain employees amongst knowledge-based companies in particular. Stock ownership is portrayed as a powerful motivational and rewards tool by consulting firms, as evidenced by the following quote from Mike Butler, the Head of Employee Ownership Consulting Practice of Hewitt Associates: '. . . It's a natural way to encourage employee loyalty. It's a way of saying "You might not work here forever, but while you're here, we expect 110%—and in return we'll share the wealth with you"' (op. cit. Greengard 1999). Supporters of stock options argue that they give employees a deserved stake in their organization—a proxy form of ownership.

More cynical observers argue that this phenomenon reflects guilty CEOs in the 1990s trying to redress the inequities of their reward in the 1980s. This perspective argues that most employees could not care less about the well-being of their company and are merely content with financial windfalls. Employees may view shares as simply a source of income, thereby undermining the 'shared ownership' concept: '. . . Employee ownership through financial participation shares money and on its own is unlikely to give rise to a greater commitment on the part of the individual employee to the interests of the organization' (Gennard & Judge 1999, p. 198). Whether this is true or not, this more critical stance does force us to define exactly what we mean by employee ownership. Indeed, in the United Kingdom, the whole issue of *employee ownership through financial participation* (the stakeholding company) is seen in the context of workforce and trade union partnership. The need for more financial participation is argued in the context of existing pay inequities between senior managers and the general workforce (Monks 1998). Financial participation is not seen as an alternative to other elements of employee involvement and commitment, but as a way of recognizing the work that employees have done in creating a profitable and successful company.

In examining the impact of wider employee ownership, two important principles then should be accepted:

1. Employee ownership comes in many different forms and to different degrees. Taking stock options as an example, how much of the company do employers want in the hands of employees? Employees may have more of a stake in ownership, but do they actually need to own the organization before we see significant shifts in organizational behaviour? Typically the total amount of options that are granted represent from 10 per cent to 12 per cent of the outstanding shares (Greengard 1999). Schemes can vary from those in which ownership is widespread, to those in which stakes are marginal at best. For example, in Starbucks stock options are available to everyone working more than 20 hours a week. More than 20 000 out of 26 000 employees participate in the scheme, and received stock options are worth on average 14 per cent of annual wages. Staff turnover operates at 33 per cent of the industry norm. What level or form of employee ownership is necessary before significant changes in organizational behaviour occur?
2. It would be a mistake to believe that employee ownership is automatically good and desirable to all. The National Centre for Employee Ownership cites a consulting study by WellFeet.com (a San Francisco research company), which argues that college graduates are placing more trust in career development and training opportunities than in stock options (stock options came sixth out of eight of the most valued

economic benefits, behind health care and year-end bonuses for this group). As with most employment relationships, there will be some individuals who will take to it, others who will go along with it passively, and yet others who will shun it. This is likely to be the case with employee ownership even more so because of the level of risk that it entails. What types of employee will be the most responsive to employee ownership?

REWARD: COMPENSATION FOR WORK OR COMPENSATION FOR LIFE?

Stock options as a form of employee ownership introduce a new form of compensation lottery, but they also raise some fascinating questions about the employment relationship of the future. Again, can we turn to the IT industry as a harbinger of social trends? Oracle and Microsoft are reported to have thousands of paper millionaires, but they still stay with the company. To be sure they are tied in with continued options being granted to allow them to accumulate wealth, but they do not leave despite high personal worth. Greengard (1999) cites some extreme examples of this. Broadcom corporation saw a sixfold increase in its share price, making 75 per cent of its 800 employees millionaires. Longer term, how will employees react to this ownership lottery? For some, it is becoming a key part of their early work socialization experience. Hi-tech and Internet start-up companies now rely heavily on stock options to provide compensation. Salaries are paid far below market value, but then salary equities become irrelevant and distorted by the need to compensate for no stock option returns. This generation of workers—or rather a proportion of them—are prepared to work in two or three different start-up options for virtually nothing in the hope that the next start-up will make them some real money. This form of ownership can be attractive to employees in their twenties and thirties without home and family, who may remain because of their motivation in the work itself. The question is: Are such people motivated by money, or by the intrinsic attraction of the work? As an organization, how will you tell the difference, and will you really care?

Sparrow (2000b) has considered some questions that rewards strategists are asking as they look at younger employees. Are they really impressed by a 20 per cent pay bonus and the prospect of a good pension scheme when they look towards the future employment relationship that they will likely experience? Perhaps, but many questions arise about potential shifts in values across the generations, and all of these have a bearing on the likely outcomes that might be expected from greater employee ownership. Are higher levels of insecurity associated with a shift in the acceptable timeframe for rewards, with a tendency for more immediate reward and less deferred gratification? As employees make choices about the exchange of free time for consumerism, will they automatically trade-off or exchange more free time for less pay? What will be the impact of the increasing attractions of, cost of losing touch with, but desire to stay in touch with, a consumer society? Will the creation of increasingly productive households and processes of wealth creation outside employment (through the value of housing, inheritance of wealth from previous generations and so forth) lead to strategies of income substitution and blunt the value and incentives created by rewards from employment? Will the pursuit of job pauperizing economic growth mean that traditional careers, progression systems, and rewards expectations become the interests of an ever narrower range of people, given that young employees enter the organization later and older employees leave it earlier? Is the pauperization of many areas of employment leading to large segments of the population becoming estranged from traditional social expectations of advancement and the historically validated exchange of financial security for compliance? In order to accommodate these potential shifts in behaviour we see calls for more inventive work-sharing, new forms of wealth distribution, alternative forms of work organization, and fundamental changes in work values.

We should then expect wide individual differences in the motivation to belong to an employee-owned organization. For some, it may reflect a values-based preference and identification with the very nature of the business. For others it might reflect a delivery mechanism for a get-rich-quick career strategy. Missing profit targets and stock options can be a major trigger of job moves in the employee-owned organization. For example, in Palo Alto, home of the stock option culture, there is 20 per cent job turnover a year. Employees who perceive themselves as having a strong 'brand value' market themselves on this basis. Salary is just the starting point in the negotiation, with the real business being done around the stock options package. Some people move into the employee-owned organization just to 'see how much I am worth' (*The Economist*, 2000). However, not all employees have a strong-enough 'brand value' to negotiate significant employee ownership, and in any event the risks are greater. Employees bear the risk of low pay and inheriting a negotiated set of stock options that rapidly become worthless. The computer industry is the third largest downsizer in the United States and the telecommunications industry is the fourth largest. For some employees, working for an employee-owned organization might represent a higher-risk but quicker route to safety (in financial terms) approach to the employment relationship—an 'I have to bear the risk, but then if all is well I can get out of this sooner' type of attitude.

With such diverse expectations, the issue of psychological identification with the organization, and individual identity, will become important. Exactly how will the acculturation process so central to the psychological contract take place? Will employees in employee-owned organizations have 'strong' psychological contracts or weak ones (in terms of the potency and centrality attached to mutual expectations), and will their commitment be anything other than just financial and transactional? These are questions that we will soon have to answer.

ORGANIZATIONAL IDENTITY: EMPLOYEES AS PRODUCERS, INTERNAL CUSTOMERS OR CONSUMERS?

Identity will become an issue in employee-owned organizations. As traditional organizational forms are increasingly dismantled, hierarchies are flattened, competencies outsourced and teams empowered, the power of organizational institutions to create an identity is being diminished (Albert, Ashforth & Dutton 2000). The internal picture of 'what the organization stands for' increasingly resides within the heads of its employees, rather than in any externalized bureaucratic structures. Indeed, the transformations of organizational identity in modern organizational forms have recently formed the subject of a Special Issue of *Academy of Management Review*. Our identification with the organization is under transition, so too is our identification with our selves as employees. Are we best served as producers, internal customers or as consumers? And by 'we' do we mean me, my children, my community or society, my country?

A useful area of exploration will be that of conflicting and confused identities within the employee-owned organization. Some work has been done within the field of entrepreneurship looking at the different motivations and identities that owner-managers have for their business (Naffziger, Hornsby & Kuratko 1994). They may, for example, treat their ownership as entrepreneurs, caretakers, administrators, or exploiters. How might this translate to the broader population of employee-owners? In an analysis of some of the contradictions within the field of HRM, Legge (1998) noted some of the role confusion that employees now have. They have roles as 'producers' (under which they might be expected to resist labour intensification, lowering of costs and changes to the employment contract), as 'internal customers' (whereby the managerial prerogative to control the employment process is pursued under the need for customer responsiveness), and as 'consumers' of the profit (whereby waste through overhead and unnecessary headcount should be rejected). Of course, the cynics see the promulgation of employee roles as consumer

as simple 'gift wrapping' of a degradation of the employment relationship for the majority, and an obscuring of the less attractive aspects of this
employment deal through the subtle use of friendly sounding language
(ownership, involvement and participation). Within the organizational
behaviour field, we are more interested in the actual behavioural consequences of this role confusion. In whom do I trust most? Myself (or my
role) as producer, customer or consumer? As the destiny of employees
becomes more tightly integrated through ownership via financial participation, issues of work/life separation (shared futures with the fortunes
of the organization) and the very meaning of work will be raised. What
will be the consequence for employees in terms of role confusion, well-
being and stress levels, work values, commitment, cooperative versus
competitive behaviours?

The confusion in identities also comes hand-in-hand with an increasing
diversity of psychological contracts at work—or certainly the attitudinal
stances within these contracts towards HRM policies aimed at a performance culture, and shared risk policies and practices (Sparrow 2000a).
Not all employees seek increased financial participation or involvement
in their organization. The assumptions of generic improvements in
motivation, commitment, and engagement with the commercial process
that seem to underlie much of the popular discussion of employee ownership are by no means proven. Indeed, there are more grounds to expect
wide individual differences in the attractiveness of such a concept, and
the relevant outcomes noted above. Within this area, we need to understand the role of generational differences in work values. It was noted
above that the very high-risk financial participation arrangements in
start-up situations may only be of interest to a proportion of younger-
generation employees. Is this really so? How are the perceptions of the
employment relationship, and the desirability of new models of reward,
participation and ownership, being shaped by current changes in the
psychological contract? Cappelli (1999) supports the conclusion that
changes are not all positive. He forwards an *imaging inertia* theory. This is
based on the assumption that altered perceptions of the employment
relationship endure throughout generational cohorts. Employees will not
make decisions or judgements (in this case about employee ownership)
purely on the basis of a rational cost–benefit model. They will rely instead
on recalling previous experiences in similar situations—imaging—and
basing their decisions on what happened then. Cappelli (1999) bases this
assertion on the observation that people who experienced the hardships
of the Great Depression often felt insecure throughout their lives even
when they had become wealthy. The generation that grew up assuming
their employer was responsible for careers may similarly never forget the
waves of downsizing. Their children, the next generation of workers, may

also never forget. Do they apply a different set of images to the issue of employee ownership, and the different role identities that exist within this? Are they more or less susceptible to the demands that shared wealth can create (images of super-rich children needing counselling to cope with their wealth come to mind here)?

Indeed, many social psychological processes—such as socialization and the creation of identity—should be expected to operate under very different contexts in employee-owned organizations. This will have important implications because these processes are associated with the formation of the psychological contract. Some examination of these processes has already begun with alternative forms of work such as telework and virtual work (Sparrow 1999). Extrapolating from this work, any examination of socialization processes into employee-owned organizations should be expected to focus on: the actual formation of a psychological contract; and the role of values fit. The option of pursuing a values fit strategy to participation in the employee-owned firm might serve as a parallel strategy to the development of a sense of identity through a strong psychological contract. If values fit exists between the employee and the employee-owned organization, then it can serve as a control mechanism (as a substitute for a strong psychological contract, or as an important precursor to the creation of one). Values fit can also serve as a way of ensuring intra-personal fit within employee owned organizations. The need to consider the different values that might serve employee-ownership moves us into the final area of this chapter—individual differences and the role of personality.

PERSONALITY: WILL THERE BE MORE OR LESS EFFECTIVE EMPLOYEE OWNERS?

Is there is a difference in a psychological sense between those aspects of personality that become important when *working for an employee-owned organization* (in each of the different role requirements that it involves), and those aspects of personality that reflect *being an effective employee organization owner*? In the previous sections it has been argued that individuals may sign up for employee ownership employment relationships for a variety of reasons—some altruistic, some fatalistic, and some highly instrumental. The impact of employee ownership on organizational behaviour will be moderated by these different contractual stances. Are some individuals more suited by personality to the higher risk/higher reward types of relationship that employee ownership entails? In this final section, I examine some of the recent work on the entrepreneurial personality or character—defined by Chell (2000) as the person who creates and pursues opportunities for capital accumulation and wealth creation—to see if individual differences might become an important element in understanding the attractiveness of employee ownership. A Special Issue on the topic has recently appeared in the *European Journal of Work and Organizational Psychology*. A series of distinctive characteristics were examined, such as the ability to spot opportunities through judgement skills, having an intention to found, attention to economic value, exploitation of profit opportunities, and perceiving the potential of situations and gambling their imagination on it. These are all characteristics that organizations would probably wish that their newly 'stake-holdered' employees would possess. To what extent was personality research able to define the characteristics that led to this?

Research in the area of effective employee ownership could benefit from the learning that entrepreneurship personality researchers have gone through within their field. First, there may some parallels between the variables found to be predictive of entrepreneurial character and variables that will play a role in examining employee-ownership behaviour. Second, the evolution of methodological stances in entrepreneurship personality research itself carries lessons for how we might study employee-ownership behaviour. From the 1960s to 1980s researchers attempted to measure single traits that told entrepreneurs apart. There was some limited evidence for locus of control, independence, need for achievement, tolerance of ambiguity and risk-taking propensity to play some role. However, results were inconsistent. Whilst psychologists were attempting to identify a single personality profile, sociologists were identifying different types of entrepreneur, such as true entrepreneurs, caretakers, administrators, those who pursued lifestyle businesses but with no growth orientation, and so forth. The parallels to future research on effective employee owners—or those most likely to be attracted to this option—are very evident here. By the 1990s researchers on entrepreneurial character realized that they needed to ask a better question (Chell 2000)—What is it that owner-entrepreneurs actually do?—and only then ask: What is the role of personality in this? Identifying simple traits associated with entrepreneurship was not an easy task. Are owner-managers automatically entrepreneurs? Should people be classed as entrepreneurs if they have started a business, made a business grow, or done something particularly risky or innovative? By focusing on behavioural competencies—what effective entrepreneurs actually did— some more consistent insights did emerge. They had an efficiency orientation, an ability to see and act on opportunity, commitment to the work contract, and showed initiative and assertiveness (McClelland 1987). The opportunistic, innovative, proactive, resourceful and imaginative categories of behaviour emerged and assessment centres were found to be a useful tool to distinguish high growth orientation entrepreneurs (Busenitx 1996; Chell 2000; Chell, Harworth & Brearley 1991; Crant 1996). The direction taken by the most recent research on entrepreneurial character should prove fruitful for adaptation to looking at effective employee-ownership behaviour. It is examining personality from a more social and cognitive perspective, examining how effective entrepreneurs make sense of their world (the constructs that they use to encode their world, the expectancies and values that they have), and how they position themselves in a network of business relationships. This strand of research is showing that there are differences in the way that they construct time and in their horizons and envisioning space (Chell, Hedberg & Miettinen 1997; Fischer et al. 1997).

CONCLUSION

To conclude, a brief examination of the psychology of employee ownership suggests that we should study a range of issues. First, we should consider whether it actually does have any impact on motivation, commitment, and involvement, and whether it deals with historical issues of fairness and equity in reward, or creates its own set of new equity issues. Second, what are the different motivations or attitudinal stances to shared ownership across the workforce, how do they pattern across key demographic groups, and how do they impact various stages of the psychological contract formation process? Third, what will be the impact on rewards behaviour? Fourth, what will be the impact on an individual's organizational identity, and what role conflicts both within the organization, and across the work-life divide, will be generated by employee ownership? Fifth, what are the dysfunctions in terms of life adjustment that might result? And sixth, what is the impact of individual differences, both as a predictor of who wishes to engage in this trend and what organizational behaviour outcomes actually result?

REFERENCES

Albert, S., Ashforth, B. F. & Dutton, J. E. (2000) Organizational identity and identification: charting new waters and building new bridges. *Academy of Management Review*, **25**(1): 13–17.
Beardwell, I. & Holden, L. (1997) *Human Resource Management: A Contemporary Perspective*. London: Financial Times/Pitman.
Busenitx, L. W. (1996) Research on entrepreneurial alertness. *Journal of Small Business Management*, **34**(4): 35–44.
Cappelli, P. (1999) *The New Deal at Work: Managing the Market-Driven Workforce*. Boston, MA: Harvard Business School Press.

Chell, E. (2000) Toward researching the 'opportunistic entrepreneur': a social constructionist approach and research agenda. *European Journal of Work and Organizational Psychology*, **9**(1): 63–80.

Chell, E., Harworth, J. & Brearley, S. (1991) *The Entrepreneurial Personality: Concepts, Cases and Categories*. London: Routledge

Chell, E., Hedberg, N. & Miettinen, A. (1997) Are types of business owner-manager universal? A cross country study of the U.K., New Zealand and Finland. In R. R. Donckels and A. Miettinen (Eds), *Research in Entrepreneurship: Toward the Next Millennium*. London: Ashgate.

Crant, J. M. (1996) The proactive personality of scale as a predictor of entrepreneurial intentions. *Journal of Small Business Management*, **34**(3): 42–49

Economist (2000) The future of work: career evolution. *The Economist*, **354**(8155), 29 January: 113–115.

Fischer, E., Reuber, A. R., Hababou, M., Johnson, W. & Lee, S. (1997) The role of socially constructed temporal perspectives in the emergence of rapid-growth firms. *Entrepreneurship Theory and Practice*, **22**(2): 13–30.

Gennard, J. & Judge, G. (1999) *Employee Relations*. London: Institute of Personnel and Development.

Greengard, S. (1999) Stock options have their ups and downs. *Workforce*, **78**(12): 44–47.

Legge, K. (1998) Flexibility: the gift-wrapping of employment degradation. In P. Sparrow and M. Marchington (Eds), *Human Resource Management: The New Agenda*. London: Financial Times/Pitman.

Mahoney, C. (2000) Share the wealth—and the headache. *Workforce*, **79**(6): 119–126.

McClelland, D. C. (1987) Characteristics of successful entrepreneurs. *Journal of Creative Behaviour*, **21**(3): 219–233.

Monks, J. (1998) Trade unions, enterprise and the future. In P. Sparrow & M. Marchington (Eds), *Human Resource Management: The New Agenda*. London: Financial Times/Pitman.

Naffziger, D. W., Hornsby, J. S. & Kuratko, D. F. (1994) A proposed research model of entrepreneurial motivation. *Entrepreneurship Theory and Practice*, **(Spring)**: 29–42.

Sparrow, P. R. (1999) Teleworking and the psychological contract: a new division of labour? In K. Daniels, D. Lamond and P. Standen (Eds), *Managing Teleworkers*. London: Sage.

Sparrow, P. R. (2000a) The new employment contract. In R. Burke & C. L. Cooper (Eds), *The Organization in Crisis*. London: Basil Blackwell.

Sparrow, P. R. (2000b) International reward management. In J. Drucker and G. White (Eds), *Reward Management—A Critical Text*. London: Pitman.

CHAPTER 4

When Employees Become Owners: Can Employee Loyalty Be Bought?

Marc Orlitzky
Australian Graduate School of Management, Sydney, Australia

and

Sara L. Rynes
Department of Management & Organizations, The University of Iowa, USA

INTRODUCTION

Despite initial skepticism, United Airlines' (UAL) implementation of an employee stock option plan (ESOP) is generally considered one of the most remarkable business success stories of the 1990s. In 1994, UAL's employees (except for its flight attendants) traded an average of 15 per cent in pay cuts for 55 per cent in employee ownership of the company and three of its 12 board seats (Chandler 1996). Thus, employee ownership at UAL was not only symbolic, but also included veto power in major corporate decisions such as mergers and acquisitions (Swoboda 1999). United marked its success story with rising efficiency, falling employee complaints, increasing market share, strong profit margins, and outperformance of the S&P 500 from 1995 to 1999 (Chandler 1996; Babwin 2000). UAL's ESOP also set an example for rivals Northwest, TWA, and Delta, which shortly thereafter introduced their own employee ownership programs (though not as far-reaching as United's; Swoboda 1999). Although United is currently experiencing problems with respect to

Trends in Organizational Behavior, Volume 8. Edited by C. L. Cooper and D. M. Rousseau.
© 2001 John Wiley & Sons, Ltd.

skyrocketing fuel costs and falling customer revenues, analysts and industry insiders suggest that these difficulties are not due to growing labor tensions or disenchantment with the ESOP (Babwin 2000).

Not all companies have benefited to the same extent from employee ownership, however. At Weirton Steel, Vermont Asbestos, and Avis, for example, the introduction of ESOPs was fraught with labor tensions and confusion (Chandler 1996; Lieber 1995). This raises questions about the causes of differential performance records after the introduction of ESOPs or employee ownership schemes. What is achieved when a company turns employees into owners or increases the equity stakes of employees? Do ESOPs and other types of ownership schemes increase employee loyalty and/or firm performance? What does recent empirical evidence show? These are the questions examined in this chapter.

The chapter consists of six sections. First, types of employee ownership are delineated and broad trends in employee ownership described. Second, we cover potential advantages and disadvantages of ESOPs. Third, the main theories (French 1987; Klein 1987; Pierce, Rubenfeld & Morgan 1991; Tannenbaum 1983) of employee affect, behavior, and performance in response to implementation of ESOPs are introduced. Fourth, we synthesize the empirical evidence in light of these models and make a few theoretical extensions. The fifth section shifts to a higher level of analysis and presents the firm financial performance benefits that have been theorized to follow from the affective and behavioral models of ESOPs. Finally, the chapter concludes with a section on future research needs.

TRENDS IN EMPLOYEE EQUITY OWNERSHIP

Employees can acquire equity stakes in their companies mainly in three different ways: through employee stock ownership plans (ESOPs), stock options, or various 401(k) plans (Blasi & Kruse 1991a). An ESOP is an employee benefit plan initiated as part of the Employee Retirement Income Security Act of 1974 (ERISA). Typically, ESOPs are leveraged, which means that companies borrow money to purchase company stock for employees and pay back the loan from ongoing operating profits (Blasi & Kruse 1991a). Of the 15 000 companies that currently share ownership broadly with employees, over two-thirds do so through ESOPs (National Center for Employee Ownership 1997, 2000). US ESOPs cover almost nine million participants and control over US$210 billion in company stock. Eighty-five per cent of ESOPs are in closely held companies, with the remaining 15 per cent accounted for by publicly traded companies (National Center for Employee Ownership 2000). Employees must be fully vested after five years of service or, in the case of a graduated vesting schedule, seven years. When companies repurchase the shares upon employee departure, the value is determined by the market in publicly traded companies or by independent appraisal of the shares' fair market value in closely held companies (National Center for Employee Ownership 2000).

Generally, ESOPs have increased in popularity since ERISA was passed. Between 1980 and 1987, the number of companies using ESOPs increased from 5700 to 8200. Since then, the growth has tapered off, with approximately 11 500 companies currently offering ESOPs (Arndt & Bernstein 2000). Since 1995, the use of ESOPs appears to have decreased slightly, while new forms of employee ownership, such as employee stock purchase plans (ESPPs), have trended upwards (Hansen 1998). Increasingly, though, the US experience with traditional ESOPs has been emulated in other countries as well.

A second way to provide employee ownership is through broadly granted stock options, a method that has been used by over 200 large US corporations (National Center for Employee Ownership 2000). Well-known examples are PepsiCo, Starbucks, and DuPont, as well as most software and Internet start-ups. In 1997, at least five million employees worked for companies that offered stock options to most or all full-time employees (National Center for Employee Ownership 1997). Stock options have gained in importance because many entrepreneurs and CEOs believe that stock options build employee commitment (National Center for Employee Ownership 2000).

Forms of stock options are the previously mentioned ESPPs, in which all employees can buy stock at up to a 15 per cent discount, incentive stock options (ISOs), and non-qualified stock options (NSOs). ISOs must satisfy certain Internal Revenue Service (IRS) conditions for preferential employee tax treatment ('qualification'), such that the applicable capital gains tax rate is deferred until the option is sold. With NSOs, exercising the option incurs ordinary income tax on the spread between the share value and the price paid for it. However, NSOs allow companies to claim a tax deduction on the spread (National Center for Employee Ownership 2000), and also to provide them to stakeholders other than employees, such as charities or suppliers.

A third and increasingly popular type of employee ownership is the variety of 401(k) plans, in which many companies now match employee contributions with company stock (at between 25 per cent and 75 per cent of employee contribution) rather than cash. Today, 401(k) plans, which are the fastest-growing employee benefit plans, must not be skewed too heavily in favor of high earners. These anti-discrimination regulations often make the contribution match necessary so that lower-paid employees are motivated to participate in these plans (National Center for

Employee Ownership 2000). Private companies tend to match employee investments to their 401(k) trust with cash. Another form is the KSOP—a combination of 401(k) plans and ESOPs—wherein a leveraged ESOP can use borrowed funds as the source of capital in its matching or additional contributions to employees' savings (Blasi & Kruse 1991a).

Traditionally, company ownership was a motivational or incentive-alignment tool for the upper-executive ranks. Increasingly, however, even entry-level hires are included in these compensation schemes. Thus, although stock options and ownership were traditionally regarded as a right of a privileged organizational elite, these types of company owner-ship are increasingly seen as potential performance and retention motiva-tors for an ever-broadening employee base.

POTENTIAL ADVANTAGES AND DISADVANTAGES OF EMPLOYEE OWNERSHIP

Employee ownership comes with benefits and disadvantages for both companies and employees. The direct administrative benefits of ESOPs are straightforward. A company's contributions to an employee's trust fund (ESOT) are tax-deductible. That is, pre-tax dollars can be used to repay an ESOP loan (if the ESOP is leveraged). Furthermore, if certain conditions are met, owners of closely held businesses can sell their equity stakes and defer taxation on the gain, according to Section 1042 of the Internal Revenue Code. Even the dividends paid on the stock are tax-deductible (Blasi 1990). Tax deductions may also apply to NSOs. Further-more, employees can defer income taxes by participating in ISO schemes or 401(k) plans. Since stock options are not treated as compensation ex-penses under Financial Accounting Standards Board (FASB) rules, they do not diminish earnings. Thus, many Internet and software start-ups use equity to alleviate some of their cash constraints in the early stages of their firm's life cycle (Martin 1998).

These positive administrative effects on both company and employee taxation are generally believed to be the major motivators behind the increasing popularity of employee ownership plans (Blasi & Kruse 1991a; Gates 1998; National Center for Employee Ownership 2000). However, other forces may also be motivating greater employee ownership. For example, due to its incentive effects, employee ownership has also been suggested to increase employee identification with the company (Blasi 1988; Tannenbaum 1983). Also, because it can take five to seven years of service before many ESOPs are fully vested, ESOPs may facilitate em-ployee retention (Reichheld 1996). Reichheld (1996) delineates seven posi-tive consequences associated with increased employee retention: lower costs of hiring (recruiting fees, interviewing costs, relocation expenses); lower employee training and development costs; higher organizational efficiency and employee motivation because of lower need for supervision; more effective customer identification and recruitment; higher customer loyalty; better customer referrals; and better employee referrals.[1]

From the perspective of organizational economics (Blasi & Kruse 1991b; Speiser 1977), ESOPs may also provide value by more closely aligning the interests of agents (employees) and principals (owners) by, in essence, turning agents into principals. Especially when ESOPs facilitate more effective communication and employee participation in decision-making, information asymmetries (and thus information costs) are reduced (Conte & Svejnar 1990). Other authors argue that employee ownership also enhances 'horizontal monitoring,' which provides net savings compared with traditional 'hierarchical monitoring' costs (Bradley & Gelb 1981; Fitzroy & Kraft 1987). In addition, broad-based employee ownership makes the cooperative solution to the Prisoner's Dilemma more likely in that employee ownership can instill certain common workplace norms and greater trust (Conte & Svejnar 1990; Dawes, McTavish & Shaklee 1977; Hosmer 1995; Marens, Wicks & Huber 1999).

Some of the postulated advantages of employee ownership may not be realized, however. For example, alignment of interests may not provide motivational or performance incentives for employees because of the inherent risk of free-ridership among employee-owners, as well as poor line of sight between employee behaviors and the company's stock price (Conte & Kruse 1991; Lawler 1991). Organizational economists emphasize that firm-wide incentives may decrease the motivation levels of existing employees, who may engage in opportunistic shirking.

In addition to the disadvantages that follow from economic reasoning, employee ownership has other potential downsides as well. First and foremost, stock ownership entails risk. Despite eight years of unprecedented stock market growth, the downside risk remains real (Arndt & Bernstein 2000; Wiseman, Gomez-Mejia & Fugate 1999). For example, between April 1999 and March 2000, United Airlines' stock price has plunged by almost 50 per cent. Moreover, since ESOPs are not covered by the Pension Benefit Guaranty Corporation (PBGC), employees are not protected against any downside risk on their stock trust or, even worse, against company mortality—a risk that is exacerbated by the lack of portfolio diversification in ESOPs (Mano & Deppe 1994). For these reasons, employee ownership may have particularly adverse attitudinal effects among risk-averse employees (Wiseman, Gomez-Mejia & Fugate 1999).

---

[1] Other authors tend to be much less sanguine about the importance of loyalty, especially as it concerns the workforce (e.g. Cappelli 1999, 2000).

Similar to these psychological explanations of perceived ownership risk, Jensen & Meckling (1979) also derive negative motivational predictions from agency theory, which regards employees as risk-averse agents (Jensen & Meckling, 1976). In contrast to Fitzroy & Kraft (1987), Jensen and Meckling do not believe that horizontal monitoring will increase in the de-layered firms in which employee ownership is widespread. Rather, they argue that monitoring costs increase as a consequence of greater employee latitude combined with non-marketable asset ownership (cf. also Alchian & Demsetz 1972). Employee shares in ESOPs are not tradable, unless the employee is 55 years old or leaves the organization. The non-transferability of these equity stakes leads to a monitoring problem because 'specialists in performance evaluation' will not emerge. Consequently, shirking is likely to be more widespread, and thus monitoring will ultimately be more costly than in firms in which only the monitors are the residual claimants on the firm's cash flows (Alchian & Demsetz 1972; Jensen & Meckling 1979). Thus, Jensen & Meckling (1979) imply that company performance will fall as a consequence of non-tradable (e.g. ESOP) employee ownership.

Although legal protections against downside risk do not exist in the case of stock options, companies have often reverted to the technique of stock option repricing. Repricing reduces the original option grant price to the current fair market value of the company stock while maintaining the original vesting and expiration dates of the option (Reynolds 1999). This response to 'underwater' options is unpopular among many compensation professionals for a variety of reasons (Cook 1999). Reissuance of options at a lower price typically depresses earnings and irritates investors (Thurm & Hwang 2000). However, option repricing is commonly practiced because it is considered necessary to ensure employee retention and motivation in periods of falling stock prices (Martin 1998; Reynolds 1999; Ward 1999).

In sum, the hypothesized positive and negative effects of ESOPs, stock options, and 401(k) plans on organizational variables call for more theoretical and empirical examination of employee ownership on micro variables—i.e. employee attitudes and behaviors—since they ultimately affect firm performance. The next section provides a comprehensive review of the academic literature on attitudinal, behavioral, and performance effects of employee ownership, with particular focus on employee loyalty.

THEORIES OF EMPLOYEE AFFECT, BEHAVIOR, AND PERFORMANCE IN RESPONSE TO OWNERSHIP

Tannenbaum (1983), French (1987), Klein (1987), and Pierce, Rubenfeld & Morgan (1991) accomplished major theoretical advances in terms of thinking about employee ownership. Tannenbaum (1983) theorized that the relationships between employee ownership, organizational identification, and job satisfaction would be generally positive, although relatively weaker among employees with low authority, influence, and hierarchical status than among high-position employees. In his view, the limited power and control of low-level employees typically prevents them from perceiving their work roles and common interests with other workers as significant drivers of either personal or organizational outcomes.

In contrast, French (1987) and French & Rosenstein (1984) conceptualized employee ownership not so much as a mechanism of control that automatically raises employees' desire for influence, but rather as a financial investment. His ownership-as-investment perspective is based on research that has clearly demonstrated the financial orientation of many employee shareowners (e.g. Greenberg 1980); Hammer & Stern 1980; Rhodes & Steers 1981, and Rosen, Klein & Young, 1986). Consistent with Blasi (1990), French (1987) argues that employee ownership consistently leads to greater organizational identification, but introduces the moderating effects of employee perceptions of firm performance, superiors, and co-workers on both the linkages between employee ownership and job satisfaction and employee ownership and desire for influence. More specifically, French (1987) postulated that employee-shareowners' perceptions of superiors and co-workers as competent and honest enhance job satisfaction relatively more than among employees without shares. In contrast, when superiors and co-workers are perceived to be incompetent and dishonest, employee-shareowners are expected to call for greater decision-making influence (French 1987).

Whereas French (1987) focused mainly on employee orientation toward ownership as a means of explaining varying results, Klein (1987) focused on the paradigmatic orientation of the researcher. She contrasted and reviewed three different models of employee ownership: (1) the intrinsic satisfaction model; (2) the extrinsic satisfaction model, and (3) the instrumental satisfaction model.

The intrinsic model considers ownership in and of itself to be satisfying and ego-enhancing to employees (Long 1978a, 1978b; Tannenbaum 1983), regardless of the attributes of the particular ESOP or company under consideration. In contrast, the extrinsic satisfaction model, which had not been tested before Klein (1987), expects employee ownership to have a positive impact on commitment if the equity stake provides the employee with financial benefits. The notion that financial reward perceptions are an important contingency is analogous to French's (1987) theoretical argument that employee ownership may give rise to investor-like expectations of financial returns, rather than expectations of increased employee power or control.

Finally, Klein (1987) summarizes the instrumental satisfaction model as postulating that employee ownership influences satisfaction indirectly, via employee influence and participation in decision-making (Stein 1976), which in turn brings about greater employee commitment (French & Rosenstein 1984; Long 1979). This 'indirect effects' model of employee ownership (Tannenbaum 1983) coincides with the assumption that employee stockholders bring a control-mechanism orientation to share ownership (cf. French 1987). Thus, the instrumental satisfaction model contradicts the intrinsic satisfaction model in that increased employee participation and control must follow employee ownership before it has any consistent positive effects on employee satisfaction and loyalty.

In a theoretical review designed to explain varying research findings, Pierce, Rubenfeld & Morgan (1991) emphasized the multidimensionality of the concept of employee ownership. Their model is reproduced in Figure 4.1. These authors distinguished between formal and psychological ownership and postulated a number of moderating variables. Psychological ownership will follow from formal ownership if (1) ownership expectations (regarding equity, influence, and information) are met, (2) the instrumental (investment) orientation of the employee is low, (3) the employee-owner perceives ownership legitimacy to be high, and (4) management shows high commitment to employee ownership. Psychological ownership will, in turn, lead to greater worker integration, of which commitment is one aspect. Apart from psychological ownership and integration, one final mediating factor linking formal employee ownership with motivation and behavioral/performance responses is the emergence of group norms and behaviors.

With all its mediating variables, Pierce, Rubenfeld & Morgan's (1991) complex model suggests that variable results might well be observed in practice. The following section reviews the empirical evidence with respect to Pierce, Rubenfeld & Morgan (1991) and the other theoretical approaches discussed above.

THE EMPIRICAL EVIDENCE: CAN EQUITY BUY EMPLOYEE LOYALTY?

The following section examines the extent to which ownership has been empirically shown to enhance employee loyalty. However, first, a definition of 'loyalty' seems in order. A loyal employee is characterized by high organizational commitment, low turnover intention, and low actual turnover. Thus, loyalty has both cognitive and behavioral aspects. Organizational commitment refers to a cognitive state, while turnover is a

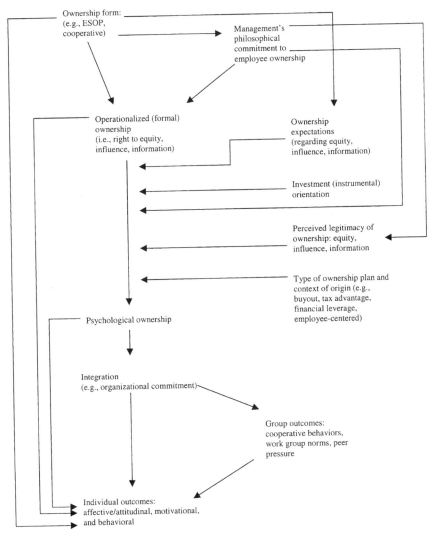

Figure 4.1 Pierce, Rubenfeld & Morgan's (1991) model of employment ownership. © Academy of Management. Reproduced with permission.

behavioral tendency (Price 1997). Certainly, organizational commitment and turnover are two distinct variables. Hence, we consider both components—commitment and turnover—in our review. Previous research shows convincingly that the relationship between commitment and turnover is substantially negative and tends to be significant, both statistically and in practice (e.g. Klein 1987; Klein & Hall 1988).

Blasi (1988) proposed that employee share ownership makes employees more committed to their jobs. The research stream that followed Blasi's (1988) 'psychological argument' cannot be considered to be a test of Pierce, Rubenfeld & Morgan's (1991) model because it does not conceptualize the construct of ownership as having two dimensions (operationalized ownership and psychological ownership). Moreover, even the research using Pierce, Van Dyne & Cummings' (1992) instrument of psychological ownership cannot be considered a rigorous test of the preconditions of how share ownership is translated into psychological ownership (Dartington 1998; Pierce, Van Dyne & Cummings 1994; Vandewalle, Van Dyne & Kostova, 1995) because it looks only at the *specific consequences* of psychological ownership, such as extra-role behaviors. Furthermore, the self-report nature of the data (e.g. Pierce, Van Dyne & Cummings, 1994; Vandewalle, Van Dyne & Kostova, 1995) means that the research may be afflicted with common-method error.

Still, there is general empirical consensus from surveys and field studies that employee ownership increases employee identification (Blasi 1988, 1990; French 1987; French & Rosenstein 1984; Hammer, Stern & Gurdon 1982; Long 1978a, 1978b, 1981; Russell, Hochner & Perry 1979). However, in contrast to Tannenbaum's prediction that employees with high authority levels would show greater increases in identification than low-authority workers, French & Rosenstein (1984) found a significantly *negative* interaction between ownership and authority with respect to organizational identification. This finding suggests that employees with relatively low formal authority exhibit greater organizational identification as a consequence of ownership.

Research on Klein's (1987) contrasting theoretical models finds relatively more support for the extrinsic and instrumental satisfaction models than the intrinsic satisfaction model. First, Klein (1987) characterizes the research stream testing intrinsic satisfaction predictions as inconsistent and inconclusive. Exemplars of intrinsic satisfaction research (e.g. French & Rosenstein 1984; Greenberg 1980; Hammer & Stern 1980; Rhodes & Steers 1981; Russell, Hochner & Perry 1979) have focused on the relationships between number of shares owned by employees (or a dichotomous 'ownership vs. no ownership' variable) and organizational identification, job satisfaction, and/or organizational commitment, either within or across companies.

Furthermore, in her own research, Klein (1987) finds no evidence of the intrinsic satisfaction effects of employee ownership. Her research in general does not show consistent significant correlations between voting rights or motivations behind ESOPs, on the one hand, and employee commitment or turnover intention, on the other. Past findings on employee ownership suggest that certain concomitant factors must exist as well. In other words, employee equity stakes do not automatically lead to 'emotional pull' and the fulfillment of employee 'fantasies' (Gross 1998, p. 70; cf. also Webb 1912). Thus, there is no evidence of a direct, unmoderated, and unmediated link from employee ownership to employee commitment, satisfaction, or turnover, which in general is consistent with Pierce, Rubenfeld & Morgan (1991).

Some of the hypothesized preconditions for the positive effects of employee ownership were tested in the context of the instrumental satisfaction model (Klein 1987). Managerial and worker perceptions of worker influence, management's philosophical commitment to employee ownership, and the extent of managerial communication about the ESOP had a consistent impact on ESOP satisfaction, commitment, and turnover intention. Yet, the existence of formal participation groups did not correlate with any of the three dependent variables (Klein 1987). Although there is no support for the importance of *all* participation mechanisms, there is some support for the instrumental satisfaction model, which proposes employee influence and commitment as mediators between ESOPs on the one hand, and satisfaction and job performance on the other.

The validity of the extrinsic satisfaction model has been demonstrated in multiple regression equations at organizational (Klein 1987) and individual levels of analysis (Klein & Hall 1988). In addition, Buchko (1992, 1993) tested the instrumental and extrinsic satisfaction models of employee ownership using longitudinal data. Multiple regression analyses found similar support for the extrinsic satisfaction model (i.e. financial value of the ESOP) as well as the instrumental satisfaction model (i.e. perceived influence) of ESOP satisfaction and organizational commitment (Buchko 1992). Moreover, instrumental satisfaction effects were negatively and significantly related to turnover and turnover intentions, whereas extrinsic satisfaction effects were not. Additionally, when the relationships were modeled in a path analysis using structural equations, Buchko (1993) found that, consistent with the instrumental view, perceived influence from ownership was a more important determinant than financial value of the ESOP for job satisfaction, organizational commitment, and turnover. However, the financial value of the ESOP, mediated by ESOP satisfaction and organizational commitment, was also significantly negatively related to turnover intention and turnover.

Figure 4.2 summarizes the contingency factors that, according to the empirical evidence accumulated so far, heighten the causal linkage between ESOPs and loyalty.

First, participation in decision-making increases organizational commitment. It is important to note that Figure 4.2 shows formal participation as a moderator, not a mediator. If it were a mediator, then it would be a necessary component of the ownership–commitment causal link. We

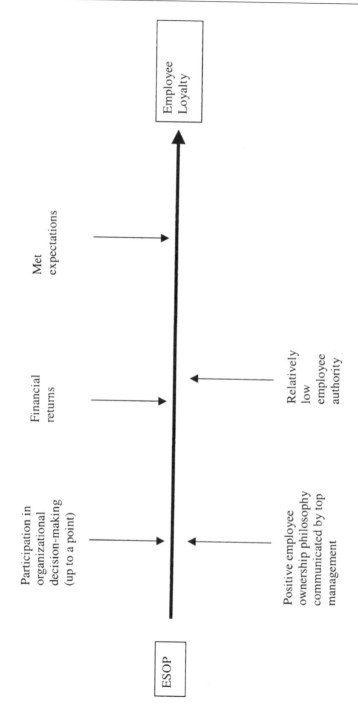

Figure 4.2   The contextual factors heightening the employee ownership–loyalty link

agree with French (1987) that there are circumstances (e.g. if a firm has high financial performance) in which employees may increase their commitment without a necessary increase in employee control over decision-making. However, consistent with Buchko's (1992, 1993) evidence, we expect the loyalty effects from employee ownership to be smaller, but not zero, when employee participation in organizational decision-making is absent. In addition, greater employee influence translates into greater job satisfaction (Buchko 1993).

Second, companies that provide satisfying financial returns to their employees are likely to enhance organizational commitment more than companies that do not. However, companies may have to strike a fine balance between employee control and the return rights held by employees (Ben-Ner & Jones 1995). At first, companies are expected to experience positive returns from increasing the shares held by employees. At a certain point, though, further ownership increases may not enhance loyalty because employees may perceive ownership as providing only minor marginal gains in psychological ownership (Pierce, Rubenfeld & Morgan 1991). In fact, at some point employees will become concerned with increasing pay risk. Although control rights and return rights are independent, organizations do not face a bifurcation point between perceptions of employee ownership as either a financial investment *or* a mechanism of control (cf. French 1987). Instead, employee ownership tends to work best when both rights coincide (Ben-Ner & Jones 1995).

Third, the commitment effects of employee ownership will depend on the extent to which the firm is able to meet employee expectations—both with respect to employees' desire for control and participation and with respect to employees' desire for financial returns from ownership. Not all employees will desire greater control in organizational decision-making (French 1987; Hammer & Stern 1980), and a variety of employee experiences will determine how high these expectations are. For example, research has found that employees who have already been laid off are more inclined toward employee ownership (Hochner & Granrose 1985). Whenever expectations are low, companies will be better able to meet them.

Fourth, top managers who not only have a comprehensive employee ownership philosophy but who also communicate their goals concerning the company's ESOPs, stock options, or 401(k) plans to employees can enhance psychological ownership relatively more and, thus, increase commitment (Klein 1987; Klein & Hall 1988; Pierce, Rubenfeld & Morgan 1991). If management can articulate how employee ownership contributes to a company's culture and identity (Gross 1998; Klein 1987; Rosen, Klein & Young 1986), then commitment is likely to be greater than when ESOPs are simply adopted as a tax-saving financial strategy.

Fifth, employee ownership increases commitment relatively more if the affected employees enjoy only low intra-organizational status or formal authority to begin with (French & Rosenstein 1984; Marens, Wicks & Huber 1999). We see this finding of an interaction, contradicting Tannenbaum's (1983) predictions, as a result of low-level employees' generally low expectations as well as their lack of alternative methods to acquire psychological ownership in the company, apart from ESOPs.

To summarize, giving employees an equity stake in their company does not automatically buy employee loyalty. A number of facilitating circumstances must exist as well to provide a significantly positive employee ownership–loyalty link. Previous research suggests that high participation, satisfactory financial returns to employees, and met expectations are the three most important moderators. However, more research needs to be undertaken to confirm certain broader economic and institutional factors of the effectiveness of employee ownership practices. For example, in a labor-market environment in which everyone offers some non-salary/non-wage compensation benefits (e.g. ESOPs, stock options, etc.) to compensate employees for leaving a previous employer, so-called 'golden handcuffs' will not work (Cappelli 2000).

Although all the preceding hypothesized effects of employee ownership on loyalty may exist (Figure 4.2), they nevertheless may not be conscious *drivers* of ESOP adoptions. As such, it is important to know the reasons given by corporate decision-makers for implementing employee ownership. In survey research, Conte, Tannenbaum & McCulloch (1981) found that, contrary to organizational–economics expectations, the main reason given (by 41 per cent of firms) for adopting ESOPs was anticipated motivational and performance incentive effects. This was followed rather closely, however, by financial (tax-incentive) effects (37 per cent).

Because social desirability may distort findings in survey research, more recent research using cross-sectional and panel data has examined objective predictors of the adoption rates of ESOPs. For example, Kruse (1996) found organizational size and capital–labor ratios to be positive predictors of the adoption and long-term maintenance of ESOPs. Moreover, although Klein (1987) found that formal participation groups had no effect on job satisfaction or organizational commitment, Kruse (1996) found that the existence of formal employee involvement programs (such as quality circles) were by far the best predictor of ESOP adoption. Other significant predictors of ESOPs were unionism (as a negative force) and variance in profit margins as a positive force (Kruse 1996). These latter results suggest that some firms use ESOPs opportunistically as a means of shifting some financial risk to employees. The specter of employee exploitation or other traditional collective mental models held by unions regarding the management–worker dichotomy may explain the unions' general opposition to ESOPs (Kruse 1996; Lindop 1989; Zalusky 1986).

EVIDENCE ON EMPLOYEE OWNERSHIP AND COMPANY PERFORMANCE

Many (probably most) employers are concerned more with the long-term, firm-level effects of ESOPS than with their short-term effects on individual attitudes and behaviors. Not surprisingly, then, company performance is the outcome variable that has attracted greatest theoretical and empirical attention over the years. Variables commonly examined in the academic literature include profitability, sales growth, employment, and productivity measures collected from various sources (e.g. surveys, public databases) and of varying degrees of sophistication. Some reviewers of the empirical literature on ESOPs and company performance have concluded that there is a relatively consistent positive link (e.g. Andrews 1996; Burzawa 1999; Marens, Wicks & Huber 1999), while others tend to be more circumspect (e.g. Blasi, Conte & Kruse 1996; Conte & Kruse 1991; Conte & Svejnar 1990; Kumbhakar & Dunbar 1993).

However, regardless of whether they perceive results to be primarily positive or mixed (e.g. Blasi, Conte & Kruse 1996), researchers agree that employee ownership interacts with employee involvement and decision-making participation to produce better company-wide results. The National Center for Employee Ownership (2000) claims on its web site that participatory ESOP firms grow 6–11 per cent faster than conventional companies (Type 4 versus Type 1 in the typology below). Evidence concerning the interaction effects of ESOPs is not conclusive, however, since information about poorly-performing ESOP firms often comes from qualitative case studies (e.g. Kruse 1984; Long 1981). Moreover, even quantitative, cross-sectional study designs sometimes do not account for all four possible combinations: (1) no ESOP/no participation; (2) ESOP, but no participation; (3) no ESOP, but participation; and (4) ESOP and participation. Notable exceptions to this failure systematically to account for all possible interactions are Hochner et al. (1988) and Winther & Marens (1997), who support the postulated positive interaction effects of ESOPs and participation (or 'communication') on company performance.

Furthermore, at least one study implies that the changes in firm performance may not simply be a Hawthorne effect in the first year after ESOP adoption (Kumbhakar & Dunbar 1993). These authors showed that generally the increase in productivity was greater in years $t + 2$ and $t + 3$, as compared with $t + 1$. Kumbhakar & Dunbar's (1993) study is noteworthy because of its rigorous estimation of firm- and time-specific effects through the use of panel data, with capital and labor elasticities allowed to vary over time. However, it falls short of some other studies (e.g. General Accounting Office 1987; Klein 1987) in terms of the specification of causal mechanisms between employee ownership and increased productivity.

Our literature review suggests that the mixed findings regarding employee ownership and firm financial performance can be explained by a variety of factors. First, many companies have not successfully implemented the conditions that facilitate the positive attitudinal and behavioral effects of employee ownership (Figure 4.2). Second, there are few longitudinal studies of employee ownership, and those that do exist often suffer from common-method variance or lack of comprehensiveness. Third, no study has systematically shown employees' cognitions (e.g. perceptions of firm performance, expectations of power sharing) leading to higher, unchanged, or lower employee motivation and performance. Finally, there has been little concern with meso research examining the effects of employee ownership at various different levels of analysis. Figure 4.3 presents a simplified diagram that depicts the various possible employee decision points.

We speculate that managerial communications and employees' perceptions of past and present company performance (relative to other similar firms) will determine the subsequent financial performance effects of ESOPs. If employees perceive company performance to be relatively high, then they will be more satisfied and have fewer changes in expectations regarding greater power sharing within the company (French 1987; Greenberg 1980; Hammer & Stern 1980; Rhodes & Steers 1981; Rosen, Klein & Young 1986). In this case, ESOPs will have no noticeable impact on individual and company performance, unless management is willing to share power with a broad base of employees (who may not have the desire for greater decision-making participation and control).

However, if company performance is perceived to be unsatisfactory, employees will develop a desire for influence and look to ESOPs not only as an investment, but also as a mechanism of control (French 1987; Hochner & Granrose 1985). Low financial performance may not be the only driver of employee expectations of power sharing, though. Employees may also develop a desire for power sharing if top management consistently communicates the desirability of more egalitarian team structures and decentralized decision-making. In this case, the significantly positive *or* negative impact of ESOPs on individual and organizational performance will be determined by the degree to which top management fulfills employee expectations through a number of participatory mechanisms. This exploratory model would even account for a possible inverted-U relationship between extent of ownership

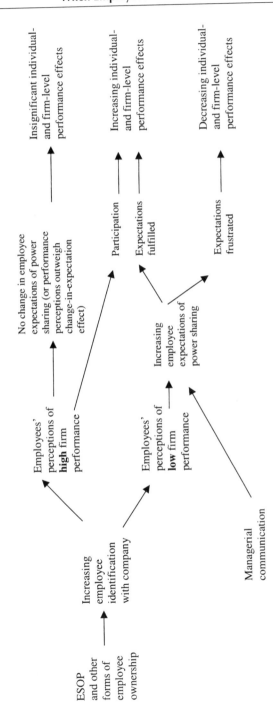

Figure 4.3 Performance effects of employee ownership

and company financial performance over time (cf. also Conte & Svejnar 1988), given that ever-greater employee control may compromise strategic decisions for which low-level employees lack competence and experience.

To summarize Figure 4.3, if (a) past and present company performance is perceived by employees to be substandard *and* (b) top management fails to communicate effectively about the company's ESOP or stock option implementation, then employees may become cynical, distrustful, and eventually leave the company (Andrews 1996; French 1987). Therefore, under certain circumstances, company equity might lead to an opposite effect from the one intended. If employee expectations of greater participation in low-performing firms are frustrated (Rosen, Klein & Young 1986), then employee ownership might have negative effects on both individual and company performance (Brooks, Henry & Livingston 1982; Livingston & Henry 1980). What is needed is a systematic investigation of the causal mechanisms linking attitudinal, behavioral, and firm-wide effects of employee ownership.

FUTURE RESEARCH NEEDS

Research on employee ownership was very active from the late 1970s to the early 1990s, but has tapered off in recent years. Apparently, some researchers have been discouraged by the variable and often weak relationships between employee ownership, employee attitudes, and company performance. However, we believe that this area still provides fertile ground for future research.

First, our two exploratory models should be tested in empirical research. For example, Figure 4.3 calls for longitudinal research with variables being measured at various crucial bifurcation points. Longitudinal research may be particularly useful because firm financial performance may have feedback effects on employee expectations about high performance and, subsequently, about power sharing. However, even in the absence of longitudinal data, Figure 4.3 suggests a clear pattern of individual and collective performance effects to be expected in a cross-sectional design.

In addition, the context of employee ownership has often changed dramatically in comparison with the contexts that were studied in the past. For example, we now need studies of the effects of employee ownership on new types of employees (e.g. software programmers) in addition to the traditional focus on blue-collar workers. Furthermore, in the future, it would be desirable to measure both psychological and financial variables so that an integrative picture of the optimal context for employee ownership can emerge. The highly variable study results of the past suggest that future studies must become more complete theoretically and operationally.[2]

Another potentially valuable approach to research on employee ownership is suggested by Gates (1998) and Marens, Wicks & Huber (1999). Specifically, from a theory standpoint, employee ownership can be linked to broader issues in business and society. Employee ownership may be one way to make capitalism a more meaningful and rewarding economic system for more employees by building a more trusting stakeholder relationship between owners, managers, and employees (Hosmer 1995). Overall, philosophical investigations of employee ownership may provide a fruitful path toward the 'deployed worker-capitalist' (Gates 1998, p. 95) and greater social equity (cf. also Rawls 1971). However, we must also clarify to what extent increasing employee stock ownership and options will lead to equity dilution and, thus, to possible dissatisfaction among existing shareholders. Research on employee ownership must take into account how the firm balances a variety of different groups' stakeholder claims in practice. This theoretical expansion calls for a study of the attitudes of a greater variety of stakeholders and for an exploration on the effectiveness of employee ownership relative to other firm-wide incentives, such as profit-sharing and gainsharing plans.

CONCLUSION

The present research base suggests employee ownership does not have consistent positive effects on employee motivation or firm productivity, *unless* employee expectations concerning participation in decision-making and firm financial performance are met. Ownership must be meaningful to lead to increased labor productivity. So far, little is known about the processes through which employees derive meaning from equity ownership and, thus, about the processes through which organizations can create greater meaning through ESOPs, stock options, and 401(k) plans. Most likely, the process of 'equity sensemaking' is somewhat different in these three types of employee ownership. More academic research is needed, especially for the latter two types. More generally, future research needs to combine the quality of statistical modeling and research design typically found in economic studies (e.g. Kumbhakar & Dunbar 1993) with industrial/organizational (I/O)

---

[2] Of course, before researchers embark on a comprehensive and costly search for contextual variables, it may be valuable to measure the proportion of cross-study variance that is accounted for by sampling error and measurement error alone.

psychology's deep concerns with measurement, construct validity, and the psychological mechanisms underlying relationships between employee ownership and personal and organizational outcomes.

ACKNOWLEDGMENTS

The authors gratefully acknowledge the assistance of AGSM MBA student Chun Ling (Agnes) NG. For any correspondence concerning this chapter, please contact the first author at AGSM, UNSW, Sydney NSW 2052, Australia, ph: +61 2 9931–9437; marco@agsm.edu.au.

REFERENCES

Alchian, A. A. & Demsetz, H. (1972) Production, information costs, and economic organization. *American Economic Review*, **62**: 777–795.

Andrews, K. Z. (1996) Equity compensation: a guide for the entrepreneur. *Harvard Business Review*, **74**(2): 13–14.

Arndt, M. & Bernstein, A. (2000) From milestone to millstone? UAL's employees are rethinking their landmark ESOP. *Business Week*, **3673**: 120–122.

Babwin, D. (2000) United air chief optimistic. Associated Press. (Internet: http://biz.yahoo.com/apf/000217/united_out_1.html).

Ben-Ner, A. & Jones, D. C. (1995) Employee participation, ownership, and productivity: a theoretical framework. *Industrial Relations*, **34**: 532–554.

Blasi, J. R. (1988). *Employee Ownership: Revolution or Ripoff?* Cambridge, MA: Ballinger.

Blasi, J. R. (1990) Comments on M. A. Conte & J. Svejnar's 'The performance effects of employee ownership plans'. In A. S. Blinder (Ed.), *Paying for Productivity: A Look at the Evidence*. Washington, DC: Brookings Institution, pp. 172–181.

Blasi, J. R. & Kruse, D. L. (1991a) *The New Owners*. New York: HarperCollins.

Blasi, J. R. & Kruse, D. L. (1991b) Strategic problems and tactical promise: unions and employee ownership. *Labor Law Journal*, **42**(8): 498–507.

Blasi, J., Conte, M. & Kruse, D. (1996). Employee stock ownership and corporate performance among public companies. *Industrial and Labor Relations Review*, **50**: 60–79.

Bradley, K. & Gelb, A. (1981) Motivation and control in the Mondragon experiment. *British Journal of Industrial Relations*, **19**: 211–231.

Brooks, L. D., Henry, J. B. & Livingston, D. T. (1982) How profitable are employee stock ownership plans? *Financial Executive*, **50**: 32–40.

Buchko, A. A. (1992) Employee ownership, attitudes, and turnover: an empirical assessment. *Human Relations*, **45**(7): 711–733.

Buchko, A. A. (1993) The effects of employee ownership on employee attitudes: an integrated causal model and path analysis. *Journal of Management Studies*, **30**: 633–658.

Burzawa, S. (1999) ESOPs pay off for employers, as well as employees. *Employee Benefit Plan Review*, **54**(1): 46–48.

Cappelli, P. (1999) *The New Deal at Work: Managing the Market-Driven Workforce*. Cambridge, MA: Harvard Business School Press.

Cappelli, P. (2000) A market-driven approach to retaining talent. *Harvard Business Review*, **78**(1): 103–111.

Chandler, S. (1996) United we own. *Business Week*, **3467**: 40–44.

Conte, M. A. & Kruse, D. (1991) ESOPs and profit-sharing plans: do they link employee pay to company performance? *Financial Management*, **20**: 91–100.

Conte, M. A. & Svejnar, J. (1988) Productivity effects of worker participation in management, profit sharing, worker ownership of assets, and unionization in U.S. firms. *International Journal of Industrial Organization*, **6**: 139–151.

Conte, M. A. & Svejnar, J. (1990) The performance effects of employee ownership plans. In A. S. Blinder (Ed.), *Paying for Productivity: A Look at the Evidence*. Washington, DC: Brookings Institution, pp. 143–172.

Conte, M., Tannenbaum, A. S. & McCulloch, D. (1981) *Employee Ownership*. Ann Arbor, MI: Survey Research Center, Institute for Social Research, The University of Michigan.

Cook, F. W. (1999) Stand up against stock option repricing. *ACA News*, 6–8.

Dartington, T. (1998) From altruism to action: Primary task and not-for-profit organization. *Human Relations*, **51**: 1477–1493.

Dawes, R., McTavish, J. & Shaklee, H. (1977) Behavior, communication and assumptions about other people's behavior in a common dilemma situation. *Journal of Personality and Social Psychology*, **35**: 1–11.

Fitzroy, F. & Kraft, K. (1987) Profitability and profit-sharing. *Journal of Industrial Economics*, **35**: 113–130.

French, J. L. (1987) Employee perspectives on stock ownership: Financial investment or mechanism of control? *Academy of Management Review*, **12**: 427–435.

French, J. L. & Rosenstein, J. (1984) Employee ownership, work attitudes, and power relationships. *Academy of Management Journal*, **27**: 861–869.

Gates, J. (1998) *The Ownership Solution*. Reading, MA: Perseus.

General Accounting Office (1987) *Employee Stockownership Plans: Benefits and Costs of Tax Incentives for Expanding Stock Ownership*. Washington, DC: US General Accounting Office.

Greenberg, E. S. (1980) Participation in industrial decision-making and worker satisfaction: the case of producer cooperatives. *Social Science Quarterly*, **60**: 551–569.

Gross, B. (1998) The new math of ownership. *Harvard Business Review*, **76**(6): 68–74.

Hammer, T. H. & Stern, R. N. (1980). Employee ownership: implications for the organizational distribution of power. *Academy of Management Journal*, **23**: 78–100.

Hammer, T., Stern, R. & Gurdon, M. (1982) Workers' ownership and attitudes towards participation. In F. Lindenfeld & J. Rothschild-Whitt (Eds), *Workplace Democracy and Social Change*, Boston, MA: Porter Sargent, pp. 87–108.

Hansen, F. (1998) Profit sharing and ESOPs are down, but ESPPs are on the rise. *Compensation and Benefits Review*, **30**(2): 11.

Hochner, A. & Granrose, C. S. (1985) Sources of motivation to choose employee ownership as an alternative to job loss. *Academy of Management Journal*, **28**: 860–875.

Hochner, A., Granrose, C., Goode, J., Simon, E. & Appelbaum, E. (1988) *Job-Saving Strategies: Worker Buyouts and QWL*. Kalamazoo, MI: Upjohn Institute for Employment Research.

Hosmer, L. T. (1995). Trust: the connecting link between organizational theory and philosophical ethics. *Academy of Management Review*, **20**: 379–403.

Jensen, M. C. & Meckling, W. H. (1976) Theory of the firm: managerial behavior, agency costs and the ownership structure. *Journal of Financial Economics*, **3**: 305–360.

Jensen, M. C. & Meckling, W. H. (1979). Rights and production functions: an application to labor-managed firms and codetermination. *Journal of Business*, **52**: 469–506.

Klein, K. J. (1987). Employee stock ownership and employee attitudes: a test of three models. *Journal of Applied Psychology Monograph*, **72**: 319–332.

Klein, K. J. & Hall, R. J. (1988) Correlates of employee satisfaction with stock ownership: Who likes an ESOP most? *Journal of Applied Psychology*, **73**: 630–638.

Kruse, D. (1984) *Employee Ownership and Employee Attitudes: Two Case Studies*. Norwood, PA: Norwood Editions.

Kruse, D. L. (1996). Why do firms adopt profit-sharing and employee ownership plans? *British Journal of Industrial Relations*, **34**: 515–538.

Kumbhakar, S. C. & Dunbar, A. E. (1993) The elusive ESOP–productivity link. *Journal of Public Economics*, **52**: 273–283.

Lawler, E. (1991) Pay for performance: a motivational analysis. In H. Nalbantian (Ed.), *Incentives, Cooperation, and Risk Sharing*. Totowa, NJ: Rowman & Little-field, pp. 69–86.

Lawler, E. E., III. & Jenkins, G. D., Jr (1990). Strategic reward systems. In M. D. Dunnette & L. M. Hough (Eds), *Handbook of Industrial and Organizational Psychology*. Palo Alto, CA: Consulting Psychologists Press, pp. 1009–1055.

Lieber, J. (1995) *Friendly Takeover: How an Employee Buyout Saved a Steel Town*. New York: Viking Press.

Lindop, E. (1989) The turbulent birth of British profit-sharing. *Personnel Management*, **21**: 44–47.

Livingston, D. T. & Henry, J. B. (1980) The effect of employee stock ownership plans on corporate profits. *Journal of Risk and Insurance*, **47**: 491–505.

Long, R. J. (1978a) The effects of employee ownership on organizational identification, employee job attitudes, and organizational performance: a tentative framework and empirical findings. *Human Relations*, **31**: 29–48.

Long, R. J. (1978b) The relative effects of share ownership vs. control on job attitudes in an employee-owned company. *Human Relations*, **31**: 753–763.

Long, R. J. (1979) Desires for and patterns of worker participation in decision-making after conversion to employee ownership. *Academy of Management Journal*, **22**: 611–617.

Long, R. J. (1981) The effects of formal participation in ownership and decision-making on perceived and desired patterns of organizational influence: a longitudinal study. *Human Relations*, **34**: 847–876.

Mano, R. M. & Deppe, E. D. (1994) The ESOP fable: employees beware! *Compensation and Benefits Review*, **26**(6): 44+ (ProQuest).

Marens, R. S., Wicks, A. C. & Huber, V. L. (1999) Cooperating with the disempowered: using ESOPs to forge a stakeholder relationship by anchoring employee trust in workplace participation programs. *Business and Society*, **38**: 51–82.

Martin, J. (1998). Quieting the concerns of nervous workers. *Fortune*, **138**(7): 191–192.

National Center for Employee Ownership (1997) A brief introduction to employee ownership. (Internet: http://www.nceo.org/library/eo_basics.html).

National Center for Employee Ownership (2000) An overview of ESOPs, stock options, and employee ownership. (Internet: http://www.nceo.org/library/).

Pierce, J. L., Rubenfeld, S. A. & Morgan, S. (1991) Employee ownership: a conceptual model of process and effects. *Academy of Management Review*, **16**: 121–144.

Pierce, J. L., Van Dyne, L. & Cummings, L. L. (1992) Psychological ownership: a construct validation study. In M. Schnake (Ed.), *Proceedings of the Southern Management Association*. Valdosta, GA: Valdosta State University, pp. 203–211.

Pierce, J. L., Van Dyne, L. & Cummings, L. L. (1994) Psychological ownership: a conceptual and empirical analysis. Unpublished manuscript.

Price, J. L. (1997) Handbook of organizational measurement. *International Journal of Manpower*, **4**, **5**, and **6**: 303–558.

Rawls, J. (1971) *A Theory of Justice*. Cambridge, MA: The Belknap Press of Harvard University Press.

Reichheld, F. F. (1996) *The Loyalty Effect: The Hidden Force Behind Growth, Profits, and Lasting Value*. Boston, MA: Harvard Business School Press.

Reynolds, R. N. (1999) How companies deal with underwater stock options. *ACA News*, 14–16.

Rhodes, S. R. & Steers, R. M. (1981) Conventional vs. worker-owned firms. *Human Relations*, **34**: 1013–1035.

Rosen, C., Klein, K. J. & Young, K. M. (1986) *Employee Ownership in America: The Equity Solution*. Lexington, MA: Lexington Books.

Russell, R., Hochner, A. & Perry, S. E. (1979) Participation, influence, and worker ownership. *Industrial Relations*, **18**: 330–341.

Speiser, S. (1977) *A Piece of the Action: A Plan to Provide Every Family with $100,000 Stake in the Economy*. New York: Van Nostrand Reinhold.

Stein, B. A. (1976) Collective ownership, property rights, and control of the corporation. *Journal of Economic Issues*, **10**: 298–313.

Swoboda, F. (1999) United's president to step down. *The Washington Post/The Detroit News*, http://detnews.com/1999/biz/9907/11/07110006.htm.

Tannenbaum, A. (1983) Employee-owned companies. In L. L. Cummings & B. Staw (Eds), *Research in Organizational Behavior, Vol. 5*. Greenwich, CT: JAI Press, pp. 235–268.

Thurm, S. & Hwang, S. L. (2000) Firms are running out of options in dot-com land as stocks weaken. *Wall Street Journal Interactive Edition* (Internet), http://interactive.wsj.com/archive/.

Vandewalle, D., Van Dyne, L. & Kostova, T. (1995) Psychological ownership: Examination of its consequences. *Group and Organization Management*, **20**(2): 210–226.

Ward, M. (1999) Repricing: a nonexecutive pay message for the East Coast media and compensation consulting community. *ACA News*, 8–9.

Webb, C. (1912) *Industrial Cooperation: The Story of a Peaceful Revolution*. Manchester, UK: Cooperative Union.

Winther, G. & Marens, R. (1997) Participatory democracy may go a long way: comparative growth performance of employee ownership firms in New York and Washington states. *Economic and Industrial Democracy*, **18**, 393–422.

Wiseman, R. M., Gomez-Mejia, L. R. & Fugate, M. (1999) *Rethinking Compensation Risk*. Working Paper. East Lansing, MI: Michigan State University.

Zalusky, J. L. (1986) Labor's collective bargaining experience with gainsharing and profit-sharing. *IRRA 39th Annual Proceedings*. Washington, DC: IRRA, pp. 174–182.

CHAPTER 5

Achieving a Sense of Ownership Among Employees: a Critical Look at the Role of Reward Systems

Annette Cox
Manchester School of Management, UMIST, UK

INTRODUCTION

Aligning the interests of employees and business owners is a frequent focus of reward systems. But developing a sense of ownership among employees is not necessarily a primary objective set for many reward systems. Obvious exceptions include employee share schemes and forms of profit-sharing, but their use is not generally widespread in either Europe or the United States. The first section of this chapter therefore examines why employers might want to encourage a sense of ownership among employees and in what ways reward systems could be used to achieve this. The chapter then goes on to explore how the design and implementation of such systems in practice often dilutes the aims of the schemes, using research evidence of the impact that reward schemes have on employees. Finally, it focuses on often neglected elements of employee involvement and participation as critical components to make such schemes succeed.

WHY THE NEED TO FOSTER FEELINGS OF EMPLOYEE OWNERSHIP?

The principle of aligning employee interests with those of the business is frequently a central goal of reward systems. Economic theories of human

Trends in Organizational Behavior, Volume 8. Edited by C. L. Cooper and D. M. Rousseau.
© 2001 John Wiley & Sons, Ltd.

behaviour, such as agency theory, assume that the interests of owners—
'principals'—and managers and employees—'agents' are divergent and
therefore cast managers and employees as actors who have to be cajoled
or coerced into ensuring that they act in the interests of the owner(s)
(Milgrom & Roberts 1992; Rowlinson 1997). Incentive pay systems are
often prescribed as an ideal tool for this purpose. But aligning employee
interests with those of an organisation's owner could be regarded as
sufficient in itself, a simple matter of picking a pay system that most
closely reflects the owner's goals for the business. Indeed, this version of
contingency theory has a long tradition as a focus of investigation in the
reward management literature (e.g. Lupton & Gowler 1969; Bowey,
Thorpe & Hellier 1986; Gerhart & Milkovich 1990; Gomez-Mejia 1992;
Montemayor 1996; Bloom & Milkovich 1998). Why might organisations
implement reward systems that offer an element of ownership to employees and, more importantly, what do employers actually want their
workers to feel ownership of? One way of answering this question is to
review the types of reward systems often used to fulfil these types of
goals and to examine the reasons why organisations implement them.

Here we immediately encounter some variations in types of scheme
according to country of operation. Many of the most popular reward
plans are subject to national legislation since they often attract tax benefits
for both the employee and the company. For the purpose of this chapter,
comments are mostly confined to the United Kingdom, although comparisons are made with the United States and Europe where appropriate.
At first glance we can see that most surveys within the United Kingdom,
at least, reveal that reward schemes that attempt to generate a degree of
ownership for employees are quite rare; Cully et al. (1999) note that less
than a third of UK companies are likely to use any form of employee
share ownership. The purest forms of these are Employee Share Ownership Plans (ESOPs) of which there are probably less than 200 in the
United Kingdom (Pendleton et al. 1995). More popular are schemes that
distribute portions of annual profits in the form of shares to employees
(share-based profit-sharing) and savings schemes from which an employee can later use the content to buy shares at a discount (Save As You
Earn or SAYE schemes). Other schemes exist for distributing shares but
have mostly been concentrated on senior managers rather than the bulk
of the workforce. Similar schemes to distribute shares exist in other European countries and advanced forms of worker autonomy and ownership
are evident in some famous institutions such as the kibbutz system of
Israel, the self-management system of the former Yugoslavia, and worker
co-operative communities like Mondragon in Spain along with a host of
smaller co-operatives in France and Italy (see Heller 1998 for a more
detailed review of these systems). Share ownership plans themselves are

generally more popular in the United States than the United Kingdom through close links to pension provision. Even in the United States however, employee share ownership is an option for the minority (Mitchell 1995; Blair & Kruse 1999).

Applying more stringent criteria, the number of employees who actually choose to participate in the schemes is also small; with some high-profile exceptions, in the United Kingdom it is unusual to find more than 10–20 per cent of employees involved in schemes where they are required to fund the purchase of shares themselves (Hyman 1995). It is doubtful therefore whether employees actually want a stake in the business in the form that reward schemes currently offer. Evidence from Baddon et al. (1989) raises the question of whether employees want to be owners at all; in their surveys, a majority of both participants and non-participants in UK SAYE schemes actively disagreed with the idea that employees should own the companies they work for and that employees who owned shares should elect managers (p. 259). The lack of widespread adoption of these reward systems also makes it doubtful whether many employers want their employees to feel like shareholders; certainly in many smaller companies, retaining financial control of the business is a key goal for many entrepreneurs (Goss 1991; Storey 1994).

Reasons for implementing reward schemes with an element of ownership are actually quite diverse. They may include pragmatic objectives such as responding to deregulation and privatisation as experienced by UK bus companies (Pendleton et al. 1995), increasing employee earnings, or simply taking advantage of tax breaks to reduce payroll costs (Hyman 1995). However, there is another set of objectives that relates more closely to notions of creating a sense of ownership among employees. These include educating employees about the financial workings and performance of the company and reducing any perceived status differences between managers and employees (Hyman 1995; Hume 1995; Kruse 1996). Some firms allegedly aspire to increase worker identification with the goals of the company in the hope that this will be accompanied by a reduction in worker identification with any union present (Hume 1995; Kruse 1996). More specifically still, other employers have particular aspirations for employee behaviour which they intend reward systems to achieve, including the reduction of absence and labour turnover rates and improvement of productivity levels (Hume 1995; Kruse 1996). These objectives have closer associations with the notion of ownership than the pragmatic objectives listed above since they involve instilling a sense of conscientiousness and responsibility for the consequences of behaviour that is more likely to be characteristic of owners of a business. In theory, profit-sharing and share ownership plans are intended to make employees aware that taking a day off sick unless genuinely ill will affect the amount of work that is done with potential consequences for business performance. Even if individuals them-selves do not act responsibly, pressure from colleagues to prevent co-workers affecting their investment or earnings should have the same effect. Reduced quit rates can result for two reasons. First, tying employees to an organisation by stipulating that a certain amount of time must elapse before they can sell shares without incurring taxation charges operates on an instrumental level through deferring employees' departure from the com-pany. Secondly, some share schemes force employees to sell their shares on quitting the firm.

These goals on the part of the employer do not necessarily imply a desire to instil feelings of organisational ownership in employees. Rather, they could be interpreted as a desire to make employees act more respon-sibly within the confines of their current *job* and take ownership of their daily work rather than elevating them to actual proprietors of the busi-ness since participation in the schemes does not necessarily attract any additional duties connected with ownership. This is a critical point, which will recur later in discussing potential criteria of reward system design and implementation which need to be fulfilled in order to foster feelings of ownership among employees.

In practice, it is dubious how many schemes are actually implemented with ownership objectives in mind. Baddon et al. (1989) conducted a large study of both managers and employees in UK companies using inter-views and survey instruments. While gaining employees' co-operation and identification with business objectives to improve company perfor-mance was a popular aim for profit-sharing and share ownership plans, specifically enabling and encouraging employees to become shareholders and therefore owners of the businesses was much less significant with only around a third of managerial respondents selecting this as a goal of the schemes (p. 88). Even more revealing is the fact that only around one-fifth of managers using share schemes believed that making employees shareholders was one of the objectives of the schemes (p. 89). An Indus-trial Relations Services (IRS) study conducted in 1994 found that fewer than 40 per cent of firms surveyed claimed to use profit-related pay (PRP) to improve productivity or to educate employees and that the most popu-lar employer objectives for PRP were increasing wages through tax relief. Case studies of share schemes reveal that they are sometimes used as part of a desire to promote vague notions of financial participation (Wilkinson et al. 1994) or as a crisis measure to boost the productivity of an ailing company (Strauss 1998a). In the light of this mixed set of management objectives, it is therefore necessary to be slightly sceptical in evaluating the impact of these reward systems, remembering that they were not necessarily implemented with the aim of fostering a sense of ownership among employees.

THE IMPACT OF REWARD SCHEMES ON OWNERSHIP SENTIMENTS AMONG EMPLOYEES

At the outset of reviewing reward schemes for effects of 'ownership', it is important to note that comparatively little research has actually concentrated on seeking evidence of changes in employee orientation to the organisation, let alone 'ownership' *per se*. Instead, one research avenue has taken the form of comparing the performance of employee-owned enterprises with those under conventional management and shareholder control (e.g. Blasi, Conte & Kruse 1996). In Britain, the launch of the UK Employee Ownership Index has made it possible to track the performance of these organisations over time and to compare them with conventional share indices (Van de Vliet 1997). Another strand of investigation consists of econometric analyses of the impact of reward systems on productivity or the financial performance of the company (e.g. Conte & Svejnar 1990; Weitzman & Kruse 1990; Kruse 1993; Bhargava 1994).

These studies might still give an indication of the extent to which ownership sentiments have been produced among employees by the schemes if we can presume that the cumulative effect of changes in employee attitudes and behaviours is to bring about improvements in business performance, but this is a big presumption and the area is fraught with difficulties of measurement. As argued elsewhere (Pendleton, Wilson & Wright 1998; Cox 2000), the linkages between implementing a pay system, changes in employee attitudes and behaviours, and firm performance are not yet well mapped. Intervening variables such as exchange rate and prices of raw materials may cause fluctuations in productivity and financial performance beyond the influence of employee behaviour (Hyman 1995). The possibility of reverse causation, i.e. that those firms introducing ownership reward schemes may be better financial performers, remains a persistent concern in evaluating the impact of these studies. We now examine the findings of studies concerned with the impact of the reward schemes on organisational outcomes in the light of the cautions discussed above before investigating reward scheme impact on employees.

Most studies of these pay schemes have found that they have a positive but marginal effect on organisational performance. Weitzman & Kruse (1990) conducted a meta-analysis of the effects of profit-sharing schemes and concluded that they appear to have mild but beneficial effects on productivity. Bhargava (1994) identified 114 British companies across different industrial sectors that implemented profit-sharing over a 10-year period and found that the introduction of profit-sharing had positive and significant effects on profitability but that they were 'one-off effects' and not prolonged (p. 1052). Kruse (1993) investigated the effects of profit-sharing on productivity among a sample of 500 US companies, of which half operated some form of profit-sharing. He found that profit-sharing had a small positive effect on productivity as measured by sales per employee and value-added per employee, but that this fluctuated slightly after the first year of adoption (p. 68) and was likely to be implemented at a time when productivity was increasing. Nevertheless, up to one-third of the companies adopting profit-sharing plans had productivity increases that were attributable to other factors (p. 72). Cash-based profit-sharing was found to be associated with a more immediate improvement in productivity than share-based schemes, but their relative impacts over time were equivocal. Calculating value-added, however, runs into the problems of contamination of monetary measures by other influences discussed above and may not therefore be an accurate measure of productivity for the purpose of evaluating the impact of profit-sharing. The impact of share ownership plans has received less attention from scholars and results of research are mixed. Conte & Svejnar's (1990) review of extant research uncovered mixed associations between share ownership and organisational performance, while a rigorous study by Blasi, Conte & Kruse (1996) also produced inconclusive results overall but found evidence of a significant impact of the schemes on performance outcomes among smaller firms.

Evidence of the impact of reward systems on employee behaviour, such as absenteeism and retention, is more clear-cut and positive. Although it is again necessary to exercise caution in interpreting the results since external factors such as trends in employment levels may affect employee behaviour, most studies in this area attempt to control for personal characteristics which may predispose employees to leave a firm or frequent absences from work. Research evaluating the impact of profit-sharing and share option schemes on absenteeism and voluntary labour turnover rates in 52 engineering and metalworking firms in Britain showed that the existence of a profit-sharing scheme was associated with labour turnover rates of between 1 and 2 per cent lower than in firms where no such schemes were used (Wilson & Peel 1991, p. 464). On the dimension of absenteeism, the use of profit-sharing and share ownership schemes was again associated with rates at least 9 per cent lower than in other firms in the sample, with employee share ownership associated with the lowest levels of around 13 per cent (p. 465). Brown, Fakhfakh & Sessions (1999) analysed data from 127 French companies across a variety of sectors and found that the presence of both employee share ownership schemes and profit-sharing schemes was associated with significant decreases in absenteeism of at least 7 per cent.

Employee reactions to reward schemes offering ownership must similarly be approached with caution and research into these has produced more mixed findings. Evaluating schemes that allow employees to choose whether or not to participate is complicated because previously held attitudes, values and material circumstances may influence which employees choose to join the schemes. The work of Kruse (1993) and Weitzman & Kruse (1990) showed that employee attitudes to the employer improved in association with the implementation of profit-sharing schemes. In the United Kingdom, remarkably little research was conducted into the effects of PRP schemes but one case study undertaken by the author showed that employees perceived the scheme to be incomprehensible in its operation, instigated as part of aggressive cost-saving measures by a new parent company. It did not alter employees' behaviour in any way but considerably worsened employees' attitudes to management and did little to help employees identify with company goals (Cox 1999). In contrast, another UK study produced cautious support for the principle of an ESOP but little evidence of any change in worker attitudes or behaviours (Wilkinson et al. 1994). Other UK studies have produced evidence of significant positive changes in employee attitudes to the firm following participation in share ownership schemes (Bell & Hanson 1984; Fogarty & White 1988) conducted by asking employees whether their attitudes have changed. Baddon et al. (1989) found evidence that a minority of employees participating in SAYE schemes displayed more positive attitudes to their employer compared with non-participants. Pendleton, Wilson & Wright (1998) in their study of employee attitudes in employee-owned UK bus companies found that less than one-third of respondents felt like owners as a result but that a 'sense of ownership' was significantly associated with organisational commitment and satisfaction for that minority.

Investigations using a more sophisticated research design have attempted to take a longitudinal approach partly in order to ascribe any change in attitudes to the reward system itself rather than other factors (Dunn, Richardson & Dewe 1991; Keef 1998). These, however, have found a complicated set of influences on employee attitudes to share ownership. Keef (1998), researching in New Zealand, discovered that previous attitudes to the company were not linked to managers' decisions of whether to buy shares and that buying shares did not appear to improve their subsequent attitudes towards the company. Dunn, Richardson & Dewe (1991) compared participants and non-participants in SAYE plans in a manufacturing firm in the United Kingdom and found no impact of share ownership on employee attitudes but a deterioration in attitudes among non-owners over time. Significantly, the authors of both these studies alert readers to the potentially important influence of other contextual variables on employee views: recent redundancies and perceptions of company performance by Keef, and an acrimonious wage claim by Dunn, Richardson & Dewe. Other factors, such as employees' perception that they are working for a successful firm, may also be important. The picture of the impact of these reward systems on employees therefore appears muddy and there are clearly several other variables that can influence the success of the schemes. We look first at some of the inhibitors of scheme success before turning to those factors that may be prerequisites for instilling a sense of ownership through these pay systems.

INHIBITORS TO THE CREATION OF OWNERSHIP FEELINGS THROUGH REWARD SYSTEMS

Examining the operation and mechanics of schemes reveals at least three potential obstacles to the creation of a true sense of ownership among participants. First, where employees are required to make a commitment to a scheme, especially where this involves the investment of their own money, participation levels, as noted above, are often small (Hyman 1995). Participants are more likely to be managers than workers, so the number of employees who may gain a sense of ownership may be fewer than any critical mass needed to create a sense of collective ownership among the workforce. Secondly, the proportion of share capital owned by employees as a percentage of a company's total value is often small; US studies have found that the average amount of stock owned by workers is less than 20 per cent (Blasi, Conte & Kruse 1996). In the United Kingdom, regulations on share-based profit-sharing schemes set a maximum level of 5 per cent of company profits that can be used to buy shares for distribution to employees, which may reflect a desire to limit the level of employee holding due to shareholder reluctance to dilute share capital. Thirdly, the regulations for statutory UK ESOPs have been particularly complicated and strict, including time limits being set for the distribution of all shares among the workforce and stipulations that a majority of trustees must represent employees rather than managers (Pendleton et al. 1995). It therefore seems that schemes that result in a substantial element of employee ownership are less popular with employers.

For employees deciding on whether or not to join a reward scheme involving ownership, a critical determinant is likely to be the level of risk associated with it. With any real ownership there is an element of risk that the business might fail. However, there is an inevitable conflict between reducing risks of loss of investment associated with share ownership sufficiently that employees will be willing to participate and reducing it so completely that there is no perceptible link between company performance and employee gains, thus removing the force of any incentive. In the United Kingdom, reward schemes have often erred towards the latter problem, most notably in one of the most popular government promoted reward schemes of the 1990s—profit-related pay (PRP). Originally launched in 1987, additional tax breaks for employers announced in 1991 suddenly made the schemes much more attractive to them. There were basically two types. The first consisted of a genuine attempt to share profits with employees, and employees received an annual tax-free bonus dependent upon the level of profit the company made and was genuinely risk-free for employees since there was only an optional bonus at stake. The second version, also known as a 'salary sacrifice' scheme, involved up to 20 per cent of employees' wages being pooled while the tax relief received by the employer was used to maintain employee net wages at pre-scheme levels. Employees received their 'sacrificed' pay at the end of the year together with a bonus, again linked to company profits. Under the 'salary sacrifice' scheme, elements of risk for employees were suppressed in two ways. First, employees' net wages were guaranteed under the schemes and even on a weekly or monthly basis their take home pay was unaffected. Secondly, numerous means of manipulating calculations of profit fluctuations from year to year, registering schemes on an annual basis, and suspending them if profits were low, meant that employers protected employees from unpredictable changes in earnings levels. While these conditions may have been necessary to persuade enough employees to agree to the scheme (by law 80 per cent of employees from any company had to agree for a PRP scheme to be implemented), the UK government finally decided that too many organisations were simply using the schemes as a 'tax dodge' to help reduce their wage costs and gradually reduced tax relief to phase the schemes out by 2000. Under SAYE schemes, employees are permitted to cash in their savings with interest and a bonus at the end of the savings period, if the value of the shares on offer is unattractive. These regulations remove any element of risk attached to the investment and while it may encourage employees to participate in the schemes, it is hardly likely to ensure that they feel the responsibility that the owner of a business might feel to make it successful. Indeed, Baddon et al.'s (1989) research found that around 40 per cent of SAYE scheme participants tended to view it as simply another form of bonus. A final barrier to the success of the reward systems at instilling feelings of ownership derives from psychological theories of motivation.

According to Vroom's (1964) Valency–Instrumentality–Expectancy (VIE) theory, a necessary condition that must be fulfilled before employees exert any effort in pursuit of a goal is the perception of a connection between the effort they put into work and the outcome that they see—the 'line of sight' test. If we interpret the outcome as being successful and/or improved company performance, then the links between the individual's effort and organisational outcomes are not necessarily self-evident and organisational performance itself can be affected by numerous factors other than the performance of employees alone. It will be hard for individuals to feel a sense of ownership without some degree of control, or at least influence, over the business in which they have a stake. The provisions of opportunities to exert influence over company performance has been a major focus of investigation as a critical moderator of the effectiveness of reward systems to deliver a sense of ownership, and the final section of this chapter consists of an analysis of the evidence in support of this proposition and an exploration of the ways in which it might be achieved.

FACTORS FOSTERING A SENSE OF EMPLOYEE OWNERSHIP FROM REWARD SYSTEMS

It is increasingly commonly accepted that in order to persuade employees to behave like owners, financial participation schemes alone are insufficient, but must be accompanied by mechanisms through which to influence decision-making power. One of the most comprehensive studies carried out recently was the Employee Participation in Organisational Change (EPOC) (1998) study, a survey of 5800 managers in 10 of the European Union (EU) member states. The researchers found that managers from companies that combined share ownership and profit-sharing schemes with initiatives to delegate more responsibility to work groups and teams reported better outcomes than those from companies using reward systems alone across a range of measures including throughput, cost reduction and output levels, all of which may be regarded as evidence that workers are behaving more like owners.

Doucouliagos (1995) undertook a meta-analysis of a variety of studies investigating the impact of types of participation, both financial and non-financial, on productivity and found that while profit-sharing and worker ownership were associated with high productivity levels, the associations were stronger for firms where workers had managerial responsibility than more conventional capitalist enterprises. Levine & Tyson (1990) argue that reward systems conveying ownership are just one plank in a strategy of participation from management and need to be accompanied by single status arrangements and a long-term perspective on industrial relations by management. Conte & Svejnar's (1990) review revealed that the presence of groups which took part in decision-making at lower levels of the organisation appeared to be associated with improved organisational performance, while the presence of employee representatives on the board and the presence of voting rights were not. Perhaps most interestingly and relevant to the topic here, Pendleton et al. (1998) conducted a survey of employees at four UK employee-owned bus companies. Using the work of Pierce, Rubenfeld & Morgan (1991, cited in

Pendleton et al. 1998) they analysed the associations between employees possessing a 'sense of ownership' and attitudinal change following the buyout. The 'sense of ownership' consisted partly of satisfaction with levels of opportunity to participate in decision-making and partly of level of involvement in the buyout process. Although being a *de facto* share owner had little positive influence on employee attitudes, the instrumental elements of participation were found to be significantly associated with organisational commitment and satisfaction.

As we can see from the studies above, there is considerably less agreement and research on what constitutes participation and which forms of participation work best to instil a sense of ownership in which circumstances. Wilpert (1998) argues for an all-encompassing definition including both direct and representative forms of participation, narrow and broad scope of issues covered, and the opportunity for workers to voice opinions as individuals and in groups, while Marchington et al. (1992) developed a typology of levels of employee involvement according to the amount of influence employees were able to exert. Clearly, different components could have a different role to play in creating feelings of ownership. Downward communication from management of financial information and business performance measures in the form of briefings, newsletters and videos could signify to employees that managers respect their interest in the well-being of the company and credit them with the capacity to understand the information presented. While this may be a laudable first step, it does not give employees the opportunity to exercise any upward influence with the prospect of influencing organisational performance, although some evidence exists to suggest that managers assume that sharing financial information with employees will lead to their automatic acceptance of management priorities and decisions (Baddon et al. 1989). Employee influence could be conceptualised as taking two broad forms—direct influence over their work and operational matters, and influence over the strategic decisions taken at higher levels in the organisation. To make a difference to business outcomes and fulfil the criterion of VIE theory discussed above (Vroom 1964), it is evident that employees actually need to have a much greater say in these matters, but the appropriate scope of influence is debatable. Advanced forms of representation such as worker directors or other employee representatives with an equal influence on strategic decisions are one option. At a lower level, involving employees in problem-solving groups, quality circles or semi-autonomous work teams may give them greater power to change processes and practices with which they are most familiar and perhaps have most knowledge and interest. The circumstances in which strong and weak forms of participation are likely to be successful need careful consideration (see Strauss 1998b for a discussion). It cannot be ignored, however, that the research literature is littered with examples of involvement and participation mechanisms that have failed and that the diffusion of such practices is slow (for a discussion see, for example, Hill 1991; Marchington et al. 1992; Ichniowski et al. 1996; Strauss 1998b). Yet many claim that aside from productivity improvements for management, there are inherent benefits for employees of humanising work through more control over, and variety in, their jobs from the implementation of participation techniques. These could include higher job satisfaction and variety, greater chance of feedback, and the opportunity to acquire new skills in team work and decision-making (Wilpert 1998).

CONCLUSIONS

The potential for reward systems to foster feelings of employee ownership by themselves seems limited; evidence to date suggests that current schemes in general have low levels of participation and only a minority of participants appear to display changed attitudes and behaviours as a result. Much greater potential appears possible from combining these reward systems with participation mechanisms, and current research suggests that organisations may ultimately benefit financially as a result. Even here though a note of caution needs sounding. The scale of change required in organisational culture, systems and structures to create true feelings of employee ownership should not be underestimated and managers may need to be willing to devolve significant amounts of decision-making power to employees. More fundamentally, the amount of influence that employees seek is itself debatable. Heller (1998) reports a large-scale study of employees which revealed that employees were quite satisfied with having relatively little influence over decisions beyond the scope of their immediate work context. The extent to which employees desire decision-making power may not therefore extend as far as literal ownership of their employing organisation. Given these findings, what then are the benefits of greater ownership in whatever form for employees? Being able to do more interesting and varied work with a greater degree of autonomy over how it is organised may lead to job satisfaction, but this is an area still disputed by academics. Ownership from the employees' perspective may be preferable in a localised form as greater responsibility for their own work. Perhaps the role of reward systems and participation mechanisms in fostering employee ownership should begin with a focus on those aspects of working life closest to employees, with participation and reward mechanisms taking the work group or plant as a structural unit. This of course is founded upon the premise that work groups themselves have some degree of autonomy, so this is possibly the area at which managers need to direct attempts to share power and foster ownership.

ACKNOWLEDGEMENTS

I am grateful to Sophie Black, Christine Hutton and Mick Marchington for comments on an earlier version of this article.

REFERENCES

Baddon, L., Hunter, L., Hyman, J., Leopold, J. & Ramsay, H. (1989) *People's Capitalism? A Critical Analysis of Profit-Sharing and Employee Share Ownership*, London: Routledge.

Bell, W. & Hanson, C. (1984) *Profit Sharing and Employee Share-Holding Attitude Survey*. London: Industrial Participation Association.

Bhargava, S. (1994) Profit-sharing and the financial performance of companies: evidence from U.K. panel data. *Economic Journal*, **104**: pp.1044–1056.

Blair, M. & Kruse, D. (1999) Worker capitalists? Giving employees an ownership stake. *Brookings Review*, **17**(4): 23–30.

Blasi, J., Conte, M. & Kruse, D. (1996) Employee stock ownership and corporate performance among public companies. *Industrial and Labor Relations Review*, **50**(1): 60–80.

Bloom, M. & Milkovich, G. (1998) Relationships between risk, incentive pay and organisational performance. *Academy of Management Journal*, **41**(3): 283–297.

Bowey, A. M., Thorpe, R. & Hellier, P. (1986) *Payment Systems and Productivity*. Basingstoke: Macmillan.

Brown, S., Fakhfakh, F. & Sessions, G. (1999) Absenteeism and employee sharing: an empirical analysis based on French panel data, 1981–1991. *Industrial and Labor Relations Review*, **52**(2): 234–254.

Conte, M. & Svejnar, J. (1990) The performance effects of employee ownership plans. In A. Blinder (Ed.), *Paying for Productivity—A Look at the Evidence*. New York: Brookings Institution, pp.143–181.

Cox, A. (1999) Supporting performance? The role of variable pay systems in medium-sized enterprises (SMEs) in the engineering sector. Paper presented to BUIRA's HRM Study Group Conference 'Researching HRM: Where Are We Going?'. Cardiff Business School, 6–7 January.

Cox, A. (2000) The importance of employee participation in determining pay system effectiveness. *International Journal of Management Reviews*, **2**(4): 357–375.

Cully, M., Woodland, S., O'Reilly, A. & Dix, G. (1999) *Britain at Work—As Depicted by the 1998 Workplace Employee Relations Survey*. London: Routledge.

Doucouliagos, C. (1995) Worker participation and productivity in labor-managed and participatory capitalist firms: a meta-analysis. *Industrial and Labor Relations Review*, **49**(1): 58–77.

Dunn, S., Richardson, R. & Dewe, P. (1991) The impact of employee share ownership on worker attitudes: a longitudinal case study. *Human Resource Management Journal*, **1**(3): 1–16.

EPOC Research Group (1998) *New Forms of Work Organisation: Can Europe Realise Its Potential?—Results of a Survey of Direct Employee Participation*. Dublin: European Foundation for the Improvement of Working and Living Conditions.

Fogarty, M. & White, M. (1988) *Share Schemes: As Workers See Them.* London: Policy Studies Institute.

Gerhart, B. & Milkovich, G. (1990) Organisational differences in managerial compensation and financial performance. *Academy of Management Journal,* **33**(4): 663–691.

Gomez-Mejia, L. (1992) Structure and process of diversification, compensation strategy and firm performance. *Strategic Management Journal,* 13: 381–397.

Goss, D. (1991) *Small Business and Society.* London: Routledge.

Heller, F. (1998) Playing the devil's advocate: limits to influence sharing in theory and practice. In F. Heller, E. Pusic, G. Strauss and B. Wilpert (Eds), *Organizational Participation: Myth and Reality.* Oxford: Oxford University Press, pp. 144–189.

Hill, S. (1991) Why quality circles failed, but total quality management might succeed. *British Journal of Industrial Relations,* **29**: 541–568.

Hume, D. (1995) *Reward Management: Employee Performance, Motivation and Pay.* Oxford: Blackwell.

Hyman, J. (1995) Financial participation. In J. Hyman & G. Mason (Eds), *Managing Employee Involvement and Participation.* London: Sage.

Ichniowski, C., Kochan, T., Levine, D., Olson, C. & Strauss, G. (1996) What works at work: overview and assessment. *Industrial Relations,* **55**: 299–333.

Industrial Relations Services (1994) PRP in the 1990s: a survey of 333 employers. *Pay and Benefits Bulletin,* 2–11.

Keef, S. (1998) The causal association between employee share ownership and attitudes: a study based on the long framework. *British Journal of Industrial Relations,* **36**(1): 73–82.

Kruse, D. (1993) *Profit-Sharing: Does it Make a Difference?* Kalamazoo, MI: W. E. Upjohn Institute for Employment Research.

Kruse, D. (1996) Why do firms adopt profit-sharing and employee share ownership plans? *British Journal of Industrial Relations,* **34**(3): 515–538.

Levine, D. & Tyson, L. (1990) Participation, productivity and the firm's environment. In A. Blinder (Ed.), *Paying for Productivity: A Look at the Evidence.* New York: Brookings Institution, pp. 183–243.

Lupton, T. & Gowler, D. (1969) *Selecting a Wage Payment System.* London: Engineering Employers' Federation.

Marchington, M., Goodman, J., Wilkinson, A. & Ackers, P. (1992) *New Developments in Employee Involvement.* London: Department of Employment.

Milgrom, P. & Roberts, J. (1992) *Economics, Organization and Management.* London: Prentice-Hall International.

Mitchell, D. (1995) Profit sharing and employee ownership: policy implications. *Contemporary Economic Policy,* **13**(2): 16–26.

Montemayor, E. F. (1996) Congruence between pay policy and competitive strategy in high performing firms. *Journal of Management,* **22**(6): 889–908.

Pendleton, A., McDonald, J., Robinson, A. & Wilson, N. (1995) The impact of employee share ownership plans on employee participation and industrial democracy. *Human Resource Management Journal,* **5**(4): 44–60.

Pendleton, A., Wilson, N. & Wright, M. (1998) The perception and effects of share ownership: empirical evidence from employee buy-outs. *British Journal of Industrial Relations,* **36**(1): 99–123.

Rowlinson, M. (1997) *Organisations and Institutions.* Basingstoke: Macmillan.

Storey, D. (1994) *Understanding the Small Business Sector.* London: Routledge.

Strauss, G. (1998a) An overview. In F. Heller, E. Pusic, G. Strauss and B. Wilpert (Eds), *Organizational Participation: Myth and Reality.* Oxford: Oxford University Press, pp. 8–39.

Strauss, G. (1998b) Participation works—if conditions are appropriate. In F. Heller, E. Pusic, G. Strauss and B. Wilpert (Eds), *Organizational Participation: Myth and Reality*. Oxford: Oxford University Press, pp. 190–119.

Van de Vliet, A. (1997) ESOP's fable becomes a reality. *Management Today*, **November**: 112–114.

Vroom, V. (1964) *Work and Motivation*. New York: Wiley.

Weitzman, M. & Kruse, D. (1990) Profit sharing and productivity. In A. Blinder (Ed.), *Paying for Productivity—A Look at the Evidence*. New York: The Brookings Institution, pp. 95–141.

Wilkinson, A., Marchington, M., Ackers, P. & Goodman, J. (1994) ESOP's fables: a tale of a machine tool company. *International Journal of Human Resource Management*, **5**(1): 121–143.

Wilpert, B. (1998) A view from psychology. In F. Heller, E. Pusić, G. Strauss and B. Wilpert (Eds), *Organizational Participation: Myth and Reality*. Oxford: Oxford University Press, pp. 40–64.

Wilson, N. & Peel, M. (1991) The impact on absenteeism and quits of profit-sharing and other forms of employee participation. *Industrial and Labor Relations Review*, **44**(3): 454–468.

CHAPTER 6

Bringing Open-book Management into the Academic Line of Sight: Sharing the Firm's Financial Information with Workers

Claudia J. Ferrante and Denise M. Rousseau
Carnegie Mellon University, Pittsburgh, USA

INTRODUCTION

Money is just a way to keep score—James Garner in the film *Cash McCall*

Firm performance is increasingly dependent upon the skills, decisions and efforts of individual employees. A competitive advantage frequently is gained through factors directly impacted by workers, such as service quality, innovation, and knowledge sharing (Pfeffer 1994). This greater dependence upon employee contributions necessitates greater trust in employees to act in ways that reflect the firm's interests (Miles & Creed 1995) and corresponding broader sharing and understanding of organizational goals and performance indicators (Pfeffer 1994). The result has been the expansion of two inter-related organizational practices that serve to reinforce worker support for the firm's goals. The first practice is expanded worker ownership in their employing firms, via stock options and other instruments of ownership. This is a means of blurring the boundary between workers and owners by aligning worker interests with those of managers and traditional financial investors in the firm

Trends in Organizational Behavior, Volume 8. Edited by C. L. Cooper and D. M. Rousseau.
© 2001 John Wiley & Sons, Ltd.

(Shperling & Rousseau, Chapter 2 in this volume). The second practice, the subject of this chapter, is the dissemination of financial information—once the sole purview of investors and managers—to a broader spectrum of the firm's employees. The dissemination of information can provide feedback on the operational and financial condition of the organization and, in the process, is intended to encourage greater employee involvement in the business of the firm (Case 1995, 1998).

This chapter addresses the broad trend toward sharing a firm's financial information with workers. It describes a particular implementation of information dissemination, a set of practices referred to as open-book management (OBM), and the organizational and cultural trends that promote it (Figure 6.1). We then consider the implications of widely disseminated financial information from the perspective of organizational behavior theory and research.

ACCESS TO FINANCIAL INFORMATION IN FIRMS

Access to information regarding the firm's activities is a key facet of firm ownership (Hart 1995). Traditionally, workers and managers have differed in their ability to access and interpret the company's financial records. Property owners have the right to inspect their property and evaluate whether users have adhered to the terms of their agreement. Similarly, the owners of firms are entitled to review corporate records and monitor managerial activities. When ownership is distributed, as in the case of publicly held firms, managers often know more about the financial status of the firm than its owners do. These managers are obliged by the laws of corporate governance to act on behalf of their firm's owners (Stinchcombe 1986).

Competing forces influence access to information regarding the firm's activities. Several forces work to inhibit the dissemination of financial information. One is the incentive for managers to manipulate reported earnings to create and then meet shareholder expectations regarding profitability (e.g. to declare steady growth in profits over time while masking wide short-term fluctuations in earnings). When managers have broad control over information regarding the firm's activities, they can reduce the control shareholders exercise by filtering the information they receive (Hart 1995; Lowenstein 1996). In addition, managerial control over financial data can come at the expense of worker access to that information, enhancing the bargaining position of managers over that of workers, particularly when the workers are organized into unions.

On the other hand, a variety of trends promote greater dissemination of financial data. Standardized global accounting practices increasingly limit

Organizational Behavior Concepts	Managerial Directives	Implementation Issues

Organizational Behavior Concepts

- Path Goal Analysis

- High Performance Work Practices

- Participation

- Power/ Influence

- Performance Feedback

Managerial Directives

- Strategic Planning

- Financial Planning

Performance Drivers / Critical Numbers

- Operational and financial values that indicate if the firm is on track to meet managerial directives

- Overall operational indicators (e.g. monthly sales, new customers, billable hours, output, market share, etc.)

- Overall financial indicators (e.g. net income, sources and uses of cash, return on assets, etc.)

Distribution of Information

- Understandable: 'less is more'; define key indicators in the simplest terms possible (e.g. revenue = sales; expense = cost of material, etc.)

- Timely: disseminate information as soon as it is available (e.g. daily, weekly, monthly, etc.)

- Unbundled: provide detail at the division, department and job level (e.g. sales for the division, expenses for the department, billable hours for the job)

- Historical and forward thinking: provide actual (past) and forecasted data (future) (e.g. actual year-to-date income, budgets, forecast for the next year)

Implementation Issues

- *Top management support*

  - Values support transparency

- *Information system adequate to support collation and dissemination of financial information*

- *Supporting practices*

  - Employee stock ownership plans

  - Bonus/ incentive compensation

- *Workforce Competency*

  - Business literacy training

Figure 6.1 Components of financial information dissemination

managerial discretion in reporting financial information (e.g. O'Brian 1999). Thus, the push to provide consistent information to a firm's investors coincides with the trend toward broader dissemination of financial data to managers and workers in all levels of the firm, promoting a common frame of reference for all the parties (Case 1995; McCoy 1996). The rise of the market mentality in the United States—where more people participate in the stock market through pension plans or personal financial planning—is a function of increased workforce education levels, expanded white-collar work, and relatively weak retirement support from the government-maintained social security system (Nadler 1998; Rousseau 2000). The increasing push for business literacy among workers in both the public and private sectors is symptomatic of the wider availability and use of financial data in motivating productivity, investment, and organizational change (Case 1998). This business literacy extends to employment negotiations, where unions and management alike use access to the company books to justify their negotiating positions (Binkley 1999; Freeman & Kleiner 1999). Another factor promoting the availability of financial information is the coupling of information technology with more sophisticated accounting models (e.g. activity-based costing), which makes it possible to evaluate the discrete costs associated with a specific set of organizational activities and distribute the information more widely (Srikant & Kekre 1991). Widespread access to these analyses can reduce managerial control over financial data as well as lessen any claims that owners might have to such information.

RELEVANCE TO EXISTING ORGANIZATIONAL RESEARCH

Despite these trends, organizational researchers have paid little attention to the dissemination and use of financial information among workers, although the issue has arisen in research on related topics. In this chapter we briefly review a sample of these ideas, including psychological ownership, performance appraisal, high-involvement work practices, and change motivation.

Psychological Ownership

Just as owners have a right to access information regarding the firm, such access has been identified as a means of creating 'psychological ownership' among workers. Psychological ownership is defined as a cognitive psychological state in which an individual feels as though the target of ownership (or a piece of that target) is his or hers (Dirk, Cummings & Pierce 1995). This state is subjective and can mean that the possession becomes part of the extended self (Belk 1988). Feelings of ownership can extend to almost anything including our reputation, our work, and other people (James 1890; Dirk, Cummings & Pierce 1995). Of course, it also extends to how individuals view themselves in relation to the organizations with which they are associated. The seminal article by Pierce and his colleagues (Pierce, Rubenfeld & Morgan 1991) identified the pivotal role that objective forms of ownership (e.g. legal title, profit sharing, information sharing, and participation) play in creating psychological ownership for an individual employee or manager. In the case of psychological ownership within firms, it has been theorized that employees that experience feelings of ownership have a greater commitment to the firm and are more motivated to perform (Pierce, Rubenfeld & Morgan 1991). These feelings can also motivate workers to monitor each other's behavior, regardless of whether their personal income is at stake.

Employees in companies that are philosophically committed to employee ownership tend to experience higher levels of psychological ownership. Firms that promote employee ownership implement one or more practices that contribute to worker commitment, such as equity sharing, employee participation in decision-making, and information sharing. Higher psychological ownership is observed when several of these practices are bundled together (Klein 1987). Both the aspects of ownership that firms offer, and the reasons for adopting ownership plans involving workers, appear to impact the perception of psychological ownership (Klein & Hall 1988; Pierce, Rubenfeld & Morgan 1991).

The psychological experience of ownership can occur without actual legal ownership. Although legal ownership of firms has been increasing, some firms and workers choose to seek the benefits associated with ownership without actually creating legal claims. Typical 'substitutes' for ownership include access to financial information regarding the firm, participation in decision-making, and profit sharing. In the case of Saturn Corporation, a division of General Motors, worker participation in production planning accompanies the sharing of financial information across all organizational levels, an effective set of practices referred to internally as 'ownership for all' (Bennett 1999).

Performance Appraisal

Research on performance appraisal processes, particularly those related to management by objectives (MBO), has reported improved performance when at least some of the objectives are expressed in terms of financial outcomes for the firm. Because MBO entails performance assessment and feedback based on financial indicators, it requires firms to share financial information internally, at least at the level addressed by the objectives set for each worker or subunit of the firm.

High Involvement Work Practices (HIWP)

This phrase refers to a coherent, integrated *system* of innovative work practices, including extensive recruiting and careful selection of workers, substantial investment in worker training, flexible job definitions, problem-solving teams, gainsharing, employment security, and extensive labor–management communication. High-involvement systems demonstrate gains in productivity and quality outcomes over traditional work systems. However, a key feature of HIWP is that a set of features must co-occur for these effects to be achieved. In contrast, individual work practice innovations have no significant effect on productivity (Ichniowski, Kochan, Levine, Olson & Strauss 1996). These innovations focus on commitment rather than control in relation to the workforce. Firms that use HIWP fundamentally assume that workers understand what behavior and outcomes promote the firm's interests. However, few studies directly examine the information disseminated through HIWP. Executive programs for human resource managers—the advocates for such practices—increasingly focus upon managers with the knowledge of business and finance in order to help them more effectively argue their case (e.g. Cornell University's Center for Advanced Human Resource Studies program, Lee Dyer, personal communication). Interestingly, discussions of workplace innovations often talk about greater participation and communication, but not the content of this communication.

Motivating Change

Downsizing, restructurings, and radical organizational changes began in large scale during the 1980s, increasing rank-and-file workers' awareness of the role that market forces play in shaping their daily lives. With economic justifications frequently offered for the often-adverse changes workers experience, market factors have taken on an increased legitimacy. Research on complex change suggests that the reasons managers give for change can have powerful effects on employee acceptance and reactions to change. Bies (1986) indicates that the reasons given for change, which he refers to as 'social accounts,' are most effective when they are easily understood by workers and entail factors not directly under managerial control. When workers do not understand financial information regarding the firm, economic reasons are often interpreted as negative and not in the workers' best interests (e.g. Rousseau & Tijoriwala 1999). Greater sharing of financial information with workers on an on-going basis can make external market issues more salient to employees than has traditionally been the case, therefore making them more effective motivators of change. When shared information over time has created a sense of psychological ownership in the firm, such information can provide the basis for more effective decision-making and change implementation.

CULTURAL TRENDS SUPPORTING BROADER DISSEMINATION OF FINANCIAL INFORMATION TO WORKERS

Two cultural trends in American society are particularly supportive of broader dissemination of financial information, and both show signs of having taken root in other countries: expanding market mentality and worker access to capital, and a preference for transparency in social systems.

Expanding Market Mentality and Worker Access to Capital

After a friend advised him to learn more about the real world by reading the business press, theologian Harvey Cox observed a phenomenon he labeled 'the market as God,' where a new 'myth of origin' has formed (without the reference to the Ark or primal floods):

> Behind descriptions of market refers, monetary policy, and the convolutions of the Dow, I gradually made out the pieces of a grand narrative about the inner meaning of human history, why things had gone wrong and how to put them to right. Theologians call these myths of origins, legends of the fall, and the doctrines of sin and redemption. But here they were again, and in only thin disguise: Chronicles about the creation of wealth, the seductive temptations of statism, captivity to facelessness economic cycles, and ultimately, salvation through the advent of free markets (Cox 1999, p. 18).

American workers are increasingly aware of the functioning of economic markets and their effects both on the firm and upon them individually. The rising market mentality accompanies an increasingly blurry boundary between workers and owners. The growth of pension funds and the aging population mean that more Americans identify with the value of their asset holdings, worry about possible inflationary consequences of higher wages, and side with the financial sector in its drive for higher profit margins. Ease of access to capital markets afforded by public stock trading and customer service-oriented investment houses help make stock market participation commonplace.

Preference for Transparency and a Belief in Mutuality

In the financial sense, transparency means that business information is an accurate representation of the firm's financial state regarding a particular indicator. Another way to think of transparency is mutuality, which means that information means the same thing to all parties. A preference for transparency is a key characteristic of American society (Rousseau 2000). Because American society is pluralistic in values and beliefs, one American often cannot easily interpret the subtle cues regarding roles, responsibilities, and performance requirements sent by another of a different background. Thus, diversity results in a preference for simple social structures ('what you see is what you get') with direct and explicit communication that leaves little room for ambiguity. Because reading subtle signals is difficult in a culturally heterogeneous society, direct and explicit communication becomes societally valued and culturally accepted. Indeed, there is evidence the firms that most successfully address diversity issues in the United States are the most explicit with regard to performance expectations. Direct communication of worker and firm interests is an important basis for American employment agreements and for the creation of mutuality or agreement in the psychological contracts of worker and employer. Dissemination of financial information by the employer is a means of explicitly communicating the firm's interests to workers, while practices such as employee stock ownership and performance bonuses bring financial information to the fore and help make the firm's interests and the workers' interests the same. This shared information and incentive system creates more explicit performance requirements in the psychological contracts of American workers, in contrast to those of other nations (Rousseau & Schalk 2000). As a corollary, we expect less explicitness in the creation of psychological contracts in societies with more homogeneous values and beliefs.

In America, the rise of scientific management, which criticizes employer arbitrariness and 'unscientific' discretion, supported this preference for transparency in social interactions during the early years of the twentieth century. More recently, the push for transparency has been supported by the scientific endeavors of American industrial-organizational psychology. Since the Civil Rights Act of 1964, this field has developed a rational, scientific basis for determining criteria for hiring, firing, promotion, and incentivizing. Current trends in human resource practices toward explicit job performance criteria and two-way or even multiple (360-degree feedback) performance appraisals are consistent with a continued movement toward transparency in employment. Wide sharing of financial information throughout the firm, coupled with transparency of this information, is a logical next step.

We now turn to an outgrowth of this diffusion of market-oriented thinking and the blurred boundary between management, financial investors, and workers: open-book management practices.

OPEN-BOOK MANAGEMENT: ITS DEFINITION AND FEATURES[1]

Open-book management (OBM) is a set of organizational practices that promote and support the wider dissemination of financial information across organizational levels. Although OBM is practiced by hundreds of organizations, it has not received any significant attention from organizational scholars (Davis 1997). One goal of this chapter is to motivate a deeper understanding and interest in OBM on the part of organizational researchers.

Through OBM, employees are not only given access to financial information but also are trained to understand and use it in making day-to-day decisions. Employees are encouraged to think and act like owners of the firm, regardless of their legal title to it, rather than as simply members of the rank-and-file. In effect, the philosophy underlying OBM challenges traditional beliefs regarding employees and their relationship with employers. Businesses have used this system over the past two decades or so to share information that has traditionally been kept under lock and key (Case 1995, 1998; Barton, Shenkir & Tyson 1998).

The four primary features of OBM systems are information sharing, business literacy training, worker empowerment, and rewards.

Information Sharing

Information that is typically shared in an OBM system includes financial statements (i.e. the income statement, balance sheet, statement of cash flows, and the budget), financial indicators (e.g. gross margin, income before taxes, and return on assets), and operational indicators such as monthly sales, number of new customers, or market share. In addition, employees are given information specific to their department, workgroup, or position. In the theory of OBM, employees can access any financial information they need to make good business decisions.

---

[1] The information for this section primarily comes from two books by John Case (*Open-Book Management: The Coming Business Revolution* and *The Open-Book Experience: Lessons from Over 100 Companies Who Successfully Transformed Themselves*) and a book by Thomas L. Barton et al. (*Open-Book Management: Creating an Ownership Culture*).

Training in Business Literacy

The meaning and use of financial information usually is not obvious to employees who have no training in accounting or finance. To combat this, training is a critical means of helping employees understand what each piece of information they receive means, not only for them, but also for the company as a whole. Mechanisms for business literacy training include formal classroom instruction and game-playing. Numerous open-book companies develop their own courses tailored to their organization, while others employ the assistance of consultants to educate employees. Successful training programs appear to have two common elements: first, information is personalized according to employees' experiences and needs, and second, learning is made as much fun as possible. Foldcraft Incorporated developed a particularly creative employee education program consisting of six hour-long classroom sessions (Case 1995). In the first session, employees use their personal information to understand a balance sheet. For example, employees list their personal assets (homes, cars, etc.) and liabilities (debts). The next session introduces items on Foldcraft's financial statements, but uses chocolate chip cookies as the product. Subsequent sessions present more complex information. Finally, the last session asks individual employees about their jobs and provides examples of how their efforts contribute to the company's financial bottom line.

Games used by organizations are either designed internally or standard games such as The Great Game of Business (Case 1998). For example, Physician Sales and Service employees participate in a monthly Family Feud-like game at an offsite location (Case 1998). Employees train for the game by studying 'cheat sheets' provided by the company. Whatever format of business literacy training an open-book company chooses, the important result is that employees become knowledgeable about their company's vital financial information, understand how their company makes money, and know what they can do to help ensure its profitability (Case 1995).

Employee Empowerment

Employee empowerment in OBM systems usually follows implementation of the first two features. Once employees are given access to vital information and receive training on how to incorporate this information into their daily tasks, they should be better able to make good decisions. For example, some open-book companies expect their employees to be intimately involved in budgeting and financial planning. Individual workers are asked to investigate and determine the value for one line item on their department's budget. Through this process, employees not only learn about the budget but also take responsibility for making sure that the department complies with it. Operations at the Chick-fil-A restaurant chain provide an additional example (Case 1998). Rather than rely wholly on their managers, employees become actively involved in decisions such as product marketing, repair of broken machinery, and staffing. Another approach taken by open-book companies is to form teams that mimic companywide operations. In effect, each team operates as a company within the company. For example, teams at Published Image Incorporated (a firm providing customized newsletters for financial service organizations) include an editor, art director, salesperson, and design staff (Case 1995). Each team is responsible for client development, price negotiation, product design and supply, collection of client fees, and maintenance of financial records. As illustrated by these examples, employees of OBM companies are able to make decisions that once were reserved for managers.

Rewards

Rewarding employees for increased contributions to the firm is the fourth part of any OBM system. If firms want employees to act like owners, they must give them a stake in the success of the organization. Similar to profit-sharing plans at non-OBM companies, typically rewards are tied to the operations and financial results of the organization as a whole. However, the main distinction between traditional and OBM reward systems is that the criteria for OBM rewards are clearly identified at the beginning of each fiscal year. In contrast, the bonus pool for traditional profit-sharing arrangements is usually not decided upon or disclosed by management until after the year has ended. Employees might not be motivated by these plans if they do not have a clear understanding of how their actions affect profit-sharing decisions. Open-book employees, however, typically motivated by their bonus plans, are more likely to understand how their day-to-day efforts and decisions relate to the bonus system.

Open-book companies usually reward through bonus pools and/or employee stock ownership plans. Bonus plans typically focus on a short-term perspective, whereas stock ownership plans encourage a long-term perspective stretching over several years. Practitioners report that both appear to be effective in encouraging employee commitment to the organization and to the open-book system (Case 1995). The bonus plans constructed by open-book companies vary with respect to the basis of the bonus pool (i.e. the financial indicator used to determine the size of the pool—such as net income or return on assets), how the bonus pool is divided (e.g. per performance evaluations, as a percentage of annual pay (equally among each employee)), and how often bonuses are paid (e.g., monthly, quarterly, semiannually, or annually; Barton, Shenkir & Tyson 1998). For example, one of R. R. Donnelley's divisions uses two operational measures to determine their bonus pool and distributes a percentage of the pool to employees each quarter, based on each unit's financial performance (Case 1998). Heflin Steel Company establishes a set of profit targets for the organization as a whole and gives employees an extra day's pay for each profit target that is met (Case 1998). Regardless of the particular reward system employed, the formal goal of OBM companies is to make sure that their rewards adequately motivate employee performance by ensuring that they are generous and fair and that the criteria for receiving rewards are transparent.

Practitioners assert that these four features are crucial to a firm's success in employing OBM. It is an empirical question how these features interact, whether all are required to be present, and how the implementation of each impacts the overall success of the OBM effort. This same set of questions is raised by researchers of other systems such as high involvement work practices (Ichniowski et al. 1996). The philosophy behind OBM is that increasing workers' access to financial information and strengthening their business literacy makes them not only more likely to participate in decision-making but also more effective when they do so. Such findings are consistent with research on worker ownership practices after World War II (Tannenbaum et al. 1974) and more recent research on worker participation in decision-making (Heller et al. 1998).

The firms employing OBM vary in size (from the tiny 'mom-and-pop' store to the large global entity) and focus (e.g. manufacturing, health care, high-tech, transportation, publishing, hospitality, and service). Most of the open-book companies operate in the United States and Canada; however, organizations in Australia, Brazil, and the United Kingdom also employ the philosophy (Case 1998).

Organizations reportedly adopt OBM systems for two primary reasons: to enhance their performance and to improve employer–employee relationships (Case 1998). Once employees are making sound business decisions throughout the organization, these firms expect to experience better product/service delivery and customer service, better financial performance, greater market share, and increased productivity. Employer–employee relationships are expected to improve as trust between labor and management increases and employees experience greater organizational commitment. To confirm these expectations, however, we need rigorous organizational research on the impact and implementation of OBM.

SUPPORTING PRACTICES IN OPEN-BOOK MANAGEMENT SYSTEMS

The dissemination of financial information, in and of itself, may not be particularly effective at achieving OBM's stated goals. Rather, open-book companies use a bundle of mutually reinforcing practices to implement the philosophy. Bundles of practices are not a new concept for organizational researchers (Huselid 1995; MacDuffie 1995). Similarly, compensation often entails a bundle of discrete elements—from stock options to bonus pay—intended to compliment one another's impact on worker motivation to perform and to remain with the firm (Bloom & Milkovich 1996). The practices that provide the most support for OBM systems are those that (a) are transparent, (b) provide useful financial information, and (c) have complete 'buy-in' from senior management.

Transparent Practices

Transparency is a concept that has been inherent in the accounting and finance industries for years. For example, in the notes accompanying financial statements, organizations are careful to outline the sources of data and methods used to value accounts. This clear (transparent) presentation of information signals the accuracy and legitimacy of the statements and encourages readers to trust the decisions made to construct them. OBM systems take transparency one step further. The financial and operational indicators pertinent to employee decision-making typically are used every day (Case 1998). Some companies have gone so far as to put up 'scoreboards' of information throughout their organizations (Case 1995, 1998; Barton, Shenkir & Tyson 1998). It is difficult for employees in these companies to perform their daily tasks without seeing—and using—the information provided.

Making Financial Information Useful

Several important attributes characterize useful financial information (Case 1998). First, the information must accurately present the status of the firm's operations and be based on accepted accounting methods and procedures. Useful information also is:

- complete, i.e. it indicates how well a firm performs three activities: maintaining profitability, obtaining and using cash, and managing assets;
- timely; some organizations dispense information on a weekly or even daily basis;

- unbundled; information should be provided to the level of detail that is necessary and most useful for employees in making decisions. For example, some companies share data by division, department, and even position, helping decision-makers at each of these levels.

Finally, useful financial information is based not only upon historical data, but also includes forecasts for future operations.

Note that all of the above characteristics are somewhat meaningless if the financial information is not understandable. Open-book organizations strive to disseminate data in its simplest terms and use business literacy training to further enable its interpretation and use.

Senior Management Support

Senior management support appears to be important for a broad class of organizational changes, and OBM is one of them. In particular, support from the Chief Executive Officer (CEO) and Chief Financial Officer (CFO) is imperative. CEOs are often the largest contributors to a philosophy's success or failure. As the gatekeeper of crucial financial information, a supportive and effective CFO is also essential to a successful open-book company. CFOs should be able to communicate and explain financial information and encourage employees to use the information in their daily tasks (Barton, Shenkir & Tyson 1998).

Perhaps the largest obstacle for CFOs in publicly traded companies to overcome is their fear of violating Securities and Exchange Commission (SEC) guidelines for dissemination of financial information (Case 1998). Two OBM companies have devised policies to ensure compliance with SEC regulations. AES Corporation proclaims all of its employees to be inside traders (Case 1998). As a result, AES employees can only buy and sell corporate stock during particular trading times. Physician Sales and Service, Inc. engages in another approach, whereby consolidated financial statements are disseminated to employees only after they have been released to the public (Case 1998; Barton, Shenkir & Tyson 1998). Branch-level information is the focus for this company's OBM system, and little consolidated information is distributed to employees.

IMPACT OF DISSEMINATING FINANCIAL INFORMATION TO WORKERS ON ORGANIZATIONAL BEHAVIOR CONCEPTS AND MANAGEMENT PRACTICES

Next we consider how the dissemination of financial information relates to some key research domains and practice areas.

Path Goal Analysis

A fundamental concept in motivation since early research on worker performance has been the concept of path goal (Georgopoulos, Mahoney & Jones 1957). A building block of later motivation theories such as expectancy (Vroom 1964) and goal-setting (Locke & Latham 1990), 'path goal' refers to the link between a well-specified performance target (such as sales revenue or units produced per hour) and the job-related behaviors that directly impact that target (e.g. routine sales techniques or performance programs). When path goal units are well specified, performance is likely to follow as a function of improved task competency, fewer ineffective or wasted efforts, and better understanding of the task itself. OBM practitioners use the concept of 'line of sight' to illustrate how choosing appropriate local performance targets can promote behavior that enhances broader organizational performance. Individual path goal modeling in the context of larger firm objectives is evident in the traditional concept of scientific management, where large organization-wide tasks were broken into units that individuals could perform. However, OBM is frequently applied in settings where workers are highly interdependent and performance metrics are established for the work group or a larger subunit. Little research exists on the effects of path goal specificity for units larger than an individual worker.

High Performance Work Practices

Information sharing, employee empowerment, and rewards are critical for organizations using high performance work practices (HIWP) to boost firm performance (Huselid 1995). These practices have been shown to enhance the knowledge and skills of employees, increase employee motivation, and increase an organization's ability to retain high performers (Jones & Wright 1992; Huselid 1995). Interestingly, HIWP researchers often pay little attention to the type of information available to employees who now participate in decision-making formerly conducted by higher management. Increased communication is reported, but the content of this communication often is not. None the less, OBM is a form of high performance work practice system in which financial information sharing is integral.

Worker Participation

Role expectations, information access, and competent decision-making shape the quality of worker participation. Where workers possess little financial knowledge, they typically do not participate in decision-making, or do so ineffectively (Tannenbaum et al. 1974; Greenwood & Gonzales Santos 1992). However, disseminating financial information in the context of an OBM system fundamentally shifts the expectations regarding workers' roles by blurring the boundaries between workers and managers and between workers and owners. Importantly, it also must spur a shift toward greater worker competence in using such information in order for such participation to be effective. However, little research exists on the nature of this competence, particularly the types of knowledge and skills that are needed to be successful. We also know little about how workers react to such training, which may be inconsistent with their own personal values.

Performance Feedback

Performance feedback is a key basis for motivating workers to contribute to the firm, yet little research exists on the motivational impact of various types of feedback. First, what effects do different levels of feedback (individual, group, subunit, or firm) have on worker motivation, and under what conditions might each be effective? The extent to which performance metrics are shared across units has been identified as an important factor in motivating workers to perform in ways that benefit the firm as a whole (Goodman 2000). Performance feedback provides a mechanism for employees to evaluate their progress toward company and individual goals. Where open-book practices entail the use of common metrics, and feedback about these measures, OBM can form the basis of cooperation and sharing across individual workers and between work units. However, OBM often involves unbundled performance metrics, the indicators used can vary significantly across units within the same firm, and there is no systematic research on the consequences of this unbundling.

Power and Influence

Widely disseminated financial information is at odds with traditional concepts in organizational design, such as hierarchies of information distributed on a 'need to know' basis, harboring information as a power base (Pfeffer 1992), and perhaps most importantly upon the basic distinctions between the roles of managers and workers. Disseminating financial information and giving workers the skills to use it can alter the balance of power between workers and managers, particularly in terms of the negotiation of employment terms. Workers who understand the company books and their contribution to the bottom line can bargain quite differently than those lacking such information. These concepts provoke interesting research questions for organizational researchers to explore.

CONCLUSION

The dissemination of a firm's financial information is a means of aligning employee contributions with the firm's strategic interests and business goals, and can also motivate employees to accept organizational change initiatives (Case 1995). Open-book management practices provide a framework for more effective involvement of workers in day-to-day decisions that impact the business and promote an array of related workplace innovations such as expanded worker ownership and responsiveness to demands for organizational change.

ACKNOWLEDGMENTS

We wish to thank Jason Merante and Jessica Smith for their research assistance. H.J. Heinz II research chair provided support to the second author for the writing of this paper.

REFERENCES

Alchian, A. & Demsetz, H. (1972) Production, information costs, and economic organization. *Quarterly Journal of Economics*, **90**: 599–617.

Barley, S. & Kunda, G. (1992) Design and devotion: sources of rational and normative ideologies of control in managerial discourse. *Administrative Science Quarterly*, **37**: 363–399.

Baron, J. N., Burton, M. D. & Hannan, M. T. (1996) The road taken: origins and evolution of employment systems in emerging companies. *Industrial and Corporate Change*, **5**: 239–275.

Barton, T. L., Shenkir, W. G. & Tyson, T. N. (1998) *Open-Book Management: Creating an Ownership Culture*. Morristown: Financial Executives Research Foundation, Inc.

Belk, R. (1988) Possessions and the extended self. *Journal of Consumer Research*, **15**: 139–168.

Bennett, W. (1999) Innovation at Saturn. Presentation at the Journal of Organizational Behavior meeting, 15 November, Detroit, Michigan, USA.

Berle, A. & Mean, G. (1932) *The Modern Corporation and Private Property*. New York: Macmillan.

Berman, K. V. (1967) *Worker-owned Plywood Companies: An Economic Analysis*. Pullman: Washington State University Press.

Bernstein, P. (1979) *Workplace Democratization: Its Internal Dynamics*. New Brunswick, NJ: Transaction Books.

Bies, R. J. (1987) The predicament of injustice: The management of moral outrage. In B. M. Staw and L. L. Cummings (Eds), *Research in Organizational Behavior*, Vol. 9. Greenwich, CT: JAI Press.

Binkley, C. (1999) At some casinos, the worst enemy isn't a card counter—it's a unionist who dissects their financial failings to push for labor's goals. *Wall Street Journal*, A1, A6.

Bloom, M. C. & Milkovitch, G. T. (1996) Issues in managerial compensation. In C. L. Cooper and D. M. Rousseau (Eds), *Trends in Organizational Behavior*, Vol. 3. Chichester, UK: John Wiley.

Case, J. (1995) *Open-Book Management: The Coming Business Revolution*. New York: HarperBusiness.

Case, J. (1998) *The Open-Book Management Experience: Lessons from over 100 Companies who Successfully Transformed Themselves*. Reading, MA: Perseus Books.

Coff, R. & Rousseau, D. M. (2000) Sustainable competitive advantage from relational wealth. In C. R. Leana and D. M. Rousseau (Eds), *Relational Wealth: The Advantages of Stability in a Changing Economy*. New York: Oxford University Press.

Cox, H. (1999) The market as god. *Atlantic Monthly*, **March**: 18–23.

Davis, T. R. V. (1997) Open-book management: its promise and pitfalls. *Organizational Dynamics*, **25**: 6–20.

Dirk, K. T., Cummings, L. L. & Pierce, J. (1995) Psychological ownership in organizations: conditions under which individuals promote and resist change. Unpublished manuscript.

Donaldson, L. & Davis. J. H. (1991) Stewardship theory or agency theory: CEO governance and shareholder returns. *Australian Journal of Management*, **16**: 49–64.

Freeman, R. B. & Kleiner, M. (1999) Do unions make enterprises insolvent? *Industrial Relations Review*, **52**: 510–527.

Georgopoulos, B. S., Mahoney, G. M. & Jones, N. W. (1957) A path goal approach to productivity. *Journal of Applied Psychology*, **41**: 345–353.

Gerhart, B. & Milkovich, G., (1992) Employee compensation: research and practice. In M. Dunnette and L. Hough (Eds), *Handbook of Industrial and Organizational Psychology*. Palo Alto, CA: Consulting Psychologists Press, pp. 481–569.

Goic, S. (1999) Employees' attitudes toward employee ownership and financial participation in Croatia: Experiences and cases. *Journal of Business Ethics*, **21**: 145–155.

Goodman, P. S. (2000) *Missing Linkages: Tools for Cross-level Organizational Research*. Newbury Park, CA: Sage.

Greenwood, D. & Gonzales Santos, J. L. (1992) *Industrial Democracy as Process: Participatory Action Research in the Fagor Cooperative Group of Mondragon*. Stockholm: Arbetslivscentrum.

Hammer, T. H. & Stern, R. M. (1980) Employee ownership: implications for the organizational distribution of power. *Academy of Management Journal*, **23**: 78–100.

Hart, O. (1995) *Firms, Contracts, and Financial Structure*. Oxford: Clarendon Press.

Hart, O. & Moore, J. (1994) Property rights and the nature of the firm. *Journal of Political Economy*, **98**: 1119–1158.

Heller, F. (1998) Influence at work: a 25-year program. *Human Relations*, **51**: 1425–1456.

Heller, F., Pusic, E., Strauss, G. & Wilpert, B. (1998) *Organizational Participation: Myth and Reality*. Oxford: Oxford University Press.

Hespe, G. & Wall, T. (1976) The demand for participation among employees. *Human Relations*, **29**: 411–428.

Huselid, M. A. (1995). The impact of human resource management practices on turnover, productivity, and corporate financial performance. *Academy of Management Journal*, **38**: 635–672.

Ichniowski, C., Kochan, T. A., Levine, D., Olson, C. & Strauss, G. (1996) What works at work: overview and assessment. *Industrial Relations*, **55**: 299–333.

Ingram, P. & Simon, T. (1995) Disentangling resource dependence and institutional explanations of organizational practice: the case of organizations' adoption of flextime and work at home. *Academy of Management Journal*, **38**: 1466–1482.

James, W. (1890) *Principles in Psychology*. New York: Macmillan.

Jones, G. R. & Wright, P. M. (1992) An economic approach to conceptualizing the utility of human resource management practices. In K. Rowland and G. Ferris (Eds), *Research in Personnel and Human Resources Management*, Vol. 10. Greenwich, CT: JAI Press.

Klein, K. J. (1987) Employee stock ownership and employee attitudes: a test of three models. *Journal of Applied Psychology Monograph*, **72**: 319–332.

Klein, K. & Hall, R. J. (1988) Correlates of employee satisfaction with stock ownership: who likes an ESOP most? *Journal of Applied Psychology*, **73**: 630–638.

Kruse, D. L. (1996) Why do firms adopt profit-sharing and employee ownership plans? *British Journal of Labor Relations*, **43**: 515–538.

Leana, C. R. & Rousseau, D. M. (2000) *Relational Wealth: The Advantages of Stability in a Changing Economy*. New York: Oxford University Press.

Levinthal, D. (1988) A survey of agency models of organizations. *Journal of Economic Behavior and Organization*, **9**: 153–185.

Locke, E. A. & Latham, G. R. (1990) *A Theory of Goal Setting and Task Performance*. Englewood Cliffs, NJ: Prentice-Hall.

Lowenstein, R. (1996) Corporate governance's sorry history. *Wall Street Journal*, **18 April**.

Macaulay, S. (1963) Non-contractual relations in business: A preliminary study. *American Sociological Review*, **28**: 55–67.

MacDuffie, J. P. (1995) Human resource bundles and manufacturing performance: organizational logic and flexible production systems in the world auto industry. *Industrial and Labor Relations Review*, **48**: 197–221.

Mayer, R., Davis, J. H. & Schoorman, D. (1995) An integrative model of organizational trust. *Academy of Management Review*, **20**: 709–734.

McCoy, T. J. (1996) *Creating an 'Open-book' Organization*. New York: AMACOM.

McCraw, T. K. (1997) *Creating Modern Capitalism: How Entrepreneurs, Companies, and Countries Brought About Three Industrial Revolutions*. Cambridge, MA: Harvard Business School Press.

Miles, R. E. & Creed, W. E. D. (1995) Organizational forms and managerial philosophies: a descriptive and analytical review. In B. M. Staw and L. L. Cummings (Eds), *Research in Organizational Behavior*, Vol. 17. Greenwich, CT: JAI Press.

Moskos, C. C. & Butler, J. S. (1996) *All That We Can Be: Black Leadership and Racial Integration the Army Way*. New York: Basic Books.

Nadler, R. (1998) Stocks populi: as workers join the investing class, America may undergo a political realignment. *National Review*, **9 March**: 36–38.

Nutzinger, H. G. (1988) Employee participation by codetermination, labor law, and collective bargaining. In G. Dlugos, W. Dorow and K. Weiermair (Eds) *Management under differing labour market and employment systems*. Berlin: Walter deGruyter, pp. 301–312.

O'Brian, B. (1999) A little light reading? Try a final prospectus. *Wall Street Journal*, **33 May**: R1, R5.

Pierce, J. L., Rubenfeld, S. A. & Morgan, S. (1991) Employee ownership: a conceptual model of process and effects. *Academy of Management Review*, **16**: 121–144.

Pierce, J. L. & Furo, C. A. (1990) Employee ownership: implications for management. *Organizational Dynamics*, **18**: 32–43.

Pfeffer, J. (1992) *Managing with Power: Politics and Influences in Organizations*. Boston, MA: Harvard Business School Press.

Pfeffer, J. (1994) *Competitive Advantage Through People: Problems and Prospects for Change*. Boston, MA: Harvard Business School Press.

Pfeffer, J. (1998) *The Human Equation*. Boston, MA: Harvard Business School Press.

Pfeffer, J. & Baron, J. N. (1988) Taking the workers back out: recent trends in the structuring of employment. In B. M. Staw and L. L. Cummings (Eds), *Research in Organizational Behavior*, Vol. 12. Greenwich, CT: JAI Press.

Pfeffer, J. & Salancik, G. R. (1978) *The External Control of Organizations: A Resource Dependence Perspective*. New York: Harper & Row.

Ritter, J. A. & Taylor, L. J. (2000) Are employees stakeholders? Corporate finance meets the agency problem. In C. R. Leana and D. M. Rousseau (Eds) *Relational Wealth: The Advantages of Stability in a Changing Economy*. New York: Oxford University Press.

Rhodes, S. R. & Steer, R. M. (1981) Conventional versus worker-owned organizations. *Human Relations*, **34**: 1013–1035.

Roe, J. J. (1990) Political and legal restraints on ownership and control of public companies. *Journal of Financial Economics*, **27**: 7–41.

Rosen, C., Klein, K. J. & Young, K. M. (1986) *Employee Ownership in America*. Lexington, MA: Lexington Books.

Rousseau, D. M. (1995) *Psychological Contracts in Organizations: Understanding Written and Unwritten Agreements*. Newbury Park, CA: Sage.

Rousseau, D. M. (1996) *Managing Diversity for High Performance*. New York: Business Week Executive Briefings.

Rousseau, D. M. (2000) Psychological contracts in the United States: diversity, individualism, and associability. In D. M. Rousseau and R. Schalk (Eds), *Psychological Contracts in Employment: Cross-national Perspectives*. Newbury Park, CA: Sage.

Rousseau, D. M. & Tijoriwala, S. A. (1999) What's a good reason to change? Motivated reasoning and social accounts in organizational change. *Journal of Applied Psychology*, **84**: 514–528.

Schleifer, A. & Vishny, R. W. (1997) A survey of corporate governance. *Journal of Finance*, **52**: 737–783.

Semler, R. (1993) *Maverick: The Success Story Behind the World's Most Unusual Workplace*. New York: Time Warner Books.

Senge, P. M. (1990). *The Fifth Discipline: The Art and Practice of the Learning Organization*. New York: Doubleday.

Shamis, G. S. & Lewandowski, N. (1996) A piece of the action: when one firm offered its professionals a chance to become owners, everyone benefited. *Journal of Accountancy*, **182**: 52–54.

Smith, M. L., Pfeffer, J. & Rousseau, D. M. (2000) Patient capital: how investors contribute to (and undermine) relational wealth. In C. R. Leana and D. M. Rousseau (Eds), *Relational Wealth: Advantages of Stability in a Changing Economy*. New York: Oxford University Press.

Srikant, D. & Kekre, S. (1991). Overloaded overheads: activity-based cost analysis of material handling in cell manufacturing. *Journal of Operations Management*, **10**: 119–137.

Stern, R. J. & Hammer, T. H. (1978) Buying your job: factors affecting the success or failure of employee acquisition attempts. *Human Relations*, **31**: 1101–1117.

Stinchcombe, A. (1986) Contracts as hierarchical documents. In A. Stinchcombe and C. Heimer (Eds), *Organizational Theory and Project Management*. Oslo: Norwegian University Press, pp. 121–171.

Tannenbaum, A.S. (1983) Employee-owned companies. In B. M. Staw and L. L. Cummings (Eds), *Research in Organizational Behavior*, Vol. 15. Greenwich, CT: JAI Press, pp. 235–268.

Tannenbaum, A. S., Kavcic, B., Rosner, M., Vianello, M. & Wieser, G. (1974) *Hierarchy in Organizations: An International Comparison*. San Francisco: Jossey-Bass.

Vroom, V. (1964) *Work and Motivation*. New York: McGraw-Hill.

CHAPTER 7

Employee Stock Transfers in SMEs: Understanding an Infrequent Event

Jerome A. Katz and Pamela M. Williams
Saint Louis University, USA

INTRODUCTION

> Persons who possess sense enough to earn money have sense enough to know how to give it away—Booker T. Washington, *Up from Slavery: An Autobiography*, 1925.

At this moment in history, stock is 'in'. It is being gobbled-up by individuals, sought after by dot-com start-up entrepreneurs, and increasingly becoming *de rigeur* as part of the signing bonus for new employees in dot-coms. The use of stock offerings to employees is going through a fundamental change in purpose and approach. This change is being driven by the surging stock market and the runaway valuations of initial public offerings. Absent in this stock option boom, however, is the owner—the entrepreneur of the small to medium enterprise (SME). Their opinions, strategic goals, and view of the growth of stock as a means of recruiting and retention have been overlooked in the Internet Stock Boom.

There are several early indicators that SME owners may be reconsidering their views about offering stock to prospective employees. Thus, there is a need to develop theories *from the owners' perspective* about how offering employees stock fits into the strategies of owners. This chapter seeks to look at the current phenomenon, place it in a historical perspective, and—lacking much direct or current research on the phenomenon—look

Trends in Organizational Behavior, Volume 8. Edited by C. L. Cooper and D. M. Rousseau.
© 2001 John Wiley & Sons, Ltd.

at related theories and research to explore the resurgent phenomenon of employee stock offerings.

HISTORIES PAST AND PRESENT

Great power has historically been attributed to ownership. In the Middle Ages, the movement from serfdom to ownership reflected the 'enlightened' view that farmers working on their own would work harder than farmers working for others. This idea resurfaced in the nineteenth century among American sharecroppers after the Civil War. The Communists found the idea in Marx's nineteenth-century foundational writings on Communism and used it to nationalize business on behalf of all workers in the early twentieth century and at the end of the century invoked the same idea to dismember and disburse those same businesses among individuals.

Ownership is often seen as such a potent influence that even small amounts could have a profoundly beneficial effect on individual employees. Many stock purchase plans result in small-scale ownership. For example, among employees of publicly held firms, individual stock ownership may be in millionths of a per cent, but is still shown to have positive influences. Ownership is perceived as such a potentially powerful influence that group researchers and consultants have adopted the idea, talking about generating employee 'ownership' of ideas, changes, and initiatives as a means of assuring the success of such efforts.

As mentioned above, at this moment in history, stock is 'in'. Stock markets worldwide are seeing unprecedented growth in offerings and valuations. Interest in stock worldwide is so great that stock exchanges are developing alliances and mergers to provide investors with information and access to stocks from around the world. Stock valuations, fueled by the advent of the dot-com Internet-based firm, are reaching stratospheric heights. For example, Priceline.com, which began by offering customer-led bidding on airline seats, has a valuation greater than Delta, American, United, KLM, or TWA, although Priceline owns almost no physical assets and makes almost no profits.

The current Internet Stock Boom, which is giving such a boost to public, founder, and employee fascination with stock, is only the latest of recurring but irregular irrationalities in the marketplace (Chancellor 1999; Morris 1999). The 1600s Tulip mania resulted in bulbs being traded for castles. In the 1700s, there were stock booms around shares in France's Mississippi Company and England's South Sea Company. Even in the modern age there were booms like that of Tokyo real estate from which Japan has still not recovered in the 10 years since the bubble burst.

Amid such popular fascination with stock during the recent Internet Stock Boom, it has become an increasingly diverse tool for organizations. Manufacturing-based 'Old Economy' models, especially among publicly traded big businesses, used stock purchase plans as a way to supplement retirement savings, to link employees' performance to the organization's performance, and incidentally to tie-in employees to the firm. Flouting this convention, franchise-oriented entrepreneurs in the 1960s and 1970s, such as Frank and Dan Carney of Pizza Hut, used franchise offerings as a way to entice experts to become and remain involved. This model has recurred for centuries. The British ships defeating the Spanish Armada in 1588 were themselves franchisees of the British Crown, their franchise agreement called a *letter du marque* (Rodger 1998).

Between the Old Economy and the service based, network driven 'New Economy', there was a perception of severe dislocation among employees. As the Old Economy firms engaged in stringent downsizing to cope with the new realities of global trade and computer-driven efficiencies, they destroyed the fundamental psychological contract (Levinson 1973; Rousseau 1995) of lifelong employment and concern for the welfare of the employee (Cappelli 1999). Sadder, wiser, and more cynical about commitment, employees moved into the world shaped by the New Economy with a more instrumental attitude. In this new model loyalty indeed *could* be bought.

As unemployment in the United States fell to one of the lowest rates in its history (3.9 per cent in April 2000), a particularly acute shortage has occurred in terms of skilled employees for owners of SMEs (defined typically as less than 500 employees in the United States or less than 100 employees elsewhere). Facing opportunity for growth fueled by the growth of global trading, the advent of the Internet Stock Boom and the increased wealth flowing into stock markets, firms, and individuals' accounts, businesses faced new challenges. Essentially the challenge was to find, secure and keep qualified employees long enough for the firm to derive benefit from their employment. With such a goal the concept of offering employees stock to join the firm naturally came to the forefront once again.

FORMS OF EMPLOYEE STOCK TRANSFERS

They say, 'If you love something, let it go;
If it comes back, it's yours; that's how you know.'
It's for keeps, yeah, it's for sure
And you're ready and willing to give me more—

Christina Aguilera, *What A Girl Wants* 1999.
http://gurlpages.com/christina–a–fan/lyrics.html

In practice there are several forms of employee stock transfers, with different legal and financial structures and serving different strategic goals of the owner. For the purposes of this chapter, the focus is a narrow one, which we will call the *Start-up Offering* or SUO. This is a stock or stock option presented by SME owners to employees as part of the salary and benefits package during hiring discussions. Before going into detail about this approach, we take a moment to provide an explanation of the three major alternative ownership forms—*Stock Grants, Stock-Options*, and *Employee Stock Ownership Plans (ESOPs)*—so that the reader can recognize how SUOs compare and contrast with other forms:

Stock Grants

Stock grants are simple and straightforward. In this case a company would give the employee shares of company stock. This option is costly for the company, as it must buy the stock for the employee but costs the employee nothing outright. However, the employee must report the value of the stock as income and pay appropriate taxes. The employee can sell the stock as soon as it is granted; thus there is no long-term organizational tie created. This method is not very popular due to the costs involved and the lack of benefit the company receives. In practice, stock grants are almost useless in SMEs, because there is no open market in which to trade stock and they are difficult to value. It would be possible to use stock grants where a current or outgoing owner wishes to sell their share of the business and this was 'granted' to the employees.

Stock Options

Stock options are popular, simple, and cost the company nothing. Developed in Old Economy companies, they inspired Start-Up Offerings in New Economy firms. When giving a stock option to an employee the company gives the employee nothing more than the right to purchase stock at the current value for a specific period of time. Since the company is not purchasing the stock there is no financial cost to the company until the employee exercises the option. Additionally, many companies use vesting (traditionally a three to five year period) to tie the employee to the company and increase employee retention. In closely held companies provisions can be made for the company to buy back the stock or facilitate buying and selling of stock between employees (NCEO Overview 2000).

In 1997, a survey conducted by the human resources consulting firm of William M. Mercer, Inc. showed that stock options, once made available only to CEO's and high ranking officers, were increasingly being offered to employees at lower levels. Their study showed that 10 per cent of

America's largest 350 companies had already made broad-based stock-option grants to their employees and another 20 per cent had guidelines and were waiting for implementation (Bowles & Sunoo 1997). By the end of 1999, a study of 1352 American firms showed 32 per cent of all American firms had guidelines and 19 per cent of workers were eligible for stock-option grants (More Workers 2000). Additionally, a recent survey of all American firms by ShareData, a stock-option plan administrator, showed that while only 17 per cent of large corporations grant stock options to over half of their employees, 68 per cent of public companies with fewer than 100 workers grant stock options to all workers (Kirwan 1999). This shows a significant increase in the popularity and implementation of stock-option grants within American firms in just the past few years.

Stock options, or share options, are also on the rise in the international arena. McKnight & Tomkins (1999) show that in the United Kingdom growth in share options increased over 145 per cent from 1993 to 1995 and that share options in 1995 accounted for 41 per cent of top executive pay compared with just 26 per cent in 1993. Another study shows that not only do 90 per cent of American publicly owned firms have stock-option programs but that the practice has spread to Japan and several European countries (Greengard 1999).

Employee Stock Ownership Plans (ESOPs)

At the other end of the spectrum there are the much more complex Employee Stock Ownership Plans (ESOPs)—an approach prevalent in modern Old Economy firms. ESOPs work like a defined contribution retirement plan holding stock for the employee until retirement, disability, or death. On average ESOPs require US$50 000 for an SME to establish, as well as an additional US$10 000 to US$15 000 annually to maintain, and they require annual stock valuations (Szabo 1994; Shanney-Saborsky 1998).

Because of the costs and complexities ESOPs might seem too aggressive for SMEs. However, about 85 per cent of ESOPs exist in closely held companies and the typical ESOP firm has only 20 to 500 employees. In private companies ESOPs hold 30–40 per cent of stock with almost one-quarter of ESOPs holding majority interest in the company. While this high percentage of ownership may be surprising, it is brought about by the fact that ESOPs are used primarily as a method for succession planning to purchase stock from departing SME owners (NCEO Ownership 2000).

Overall employee stock ownership efforts have been achieved in a small percentage of the total population of organizations. Although companies in the United States, such as Starbucks, Amazon.com, Southwest Airlines, Intel, Whole Foods, PeopleSoft, Bristol-Myers Squibb, Procter & Gamble, and Microsoft offer ESOPs, only 11 000 plans exist among over 22 million US firms and those plans cover only approximately nine million of the nation's nearly 59 million workers (Rodrick 1998; US Census Bureau 1999). While precise numbers are not available, the National Center for Employee Ownership (NCEO) also reports that employees own, or have option to own, about 9 per cent of all the stock in the United States (NCEO History 2000).

While more widely used in the United Kingdom, the numbers for employee stock ownership plans are still low, with only 1200 stock option purchase plans (called ShareSave in the United Kingdom) and 3750 Company Share Option Plans (ESOPs) (Proshare 2000). Between the two approaches, aproximately two million UK employees are covered.

Start-up Offerings

Start-up Offerings (SUOs) represent a fourth alternative and one prevalent in New Economy SMEs (Nesheim 2000). Like traditional stock options, SUOs are known by employees upon signing with the firm. Unlike traditional stock option models, SUOs often begin to accrue immediately upon hiring, although like other approaches, lengthy vesting periods are the norm. Similar to ESOPs, part of the goal is to share ownership in the firm, although unlike ESOPs, SUOs are designed and positioned with the hope that the firm is either bought-out by a larger company or is one of the fortunate few who are able to float an Initial Public Offering (IPO). Either approach would permit the cashing-out of the stock and given the Internet Stock Boom, such cash-outs were funded at wildly exorbitant levels.

The SUO approach shows an instrumentality of the owner in the start-up period. Lacking financial resources and needing expertise from the firm's inception, SUOs become an alternative to hard-dollar payments (Lawrence 2000). They also serve as a means to attract and lock-in key employees, since the employee moving to another firm will forfeit the SUO. As with other approaches, SUOs are expected to motivate employees to increase their efforts to help the firms achieve a higher stock valuation (Nesheim 2000). Unlike the other two approaches, the value of stock in SUOs is entirely arbitrary. There are a myriad of accepted ways to value privately held firms (Pratt, Reilly & Schweihs 1996) and the valuation of publicly traded stock is known to the minute. For a start-up, however, with no track record and perhaps even no product, service, or customer, the value of stock in the privately held firm is difficult to assess. Its value is dependent upon the owner's ability to convince the new hire that the future firm will have sufficient value to make the stock given today worthwhile.

Especially in the technology industry stock options are being used in the recruiting stage to attract workers with 'hot skills' (Jones Thompson 1999). In a 1999 survey, PricewaterhouseCoopers LLP surveyed compensation in the American software industry and found that 64 per cent of these firms are offering stock options in the recruiting stage alone in an attempt to tie the employee to a longer future with the firm. Another recent survey from Executive Alliance reports that sales representatives in the software industry are receiving stock-option bonuses as recruitment and retention incentives in the range of 10–50 per cent of their salary (Hansen 2000).

Kirwan (1999) reports that we can blame the increase in stock-option popularity on the success of IPOs in recent years. Likewise, Burzawa (1999) notes that the emphasis on retaining good employees combined with the high stock markets have given companies a simple and less expensive way to give high compensation packages as well as an incentive to stay with the firm long term. Regardless of the cause, the fact remains that granting employees stock options is being increasingly used in large and fast growing companies to retain qualified workers. Even so, the choices available to larger companies are not always available, or practicable, for smaller companies.

From the owner's standpoint the impacts of the four approaches are substantially different. For traditional stock option and stock grant plans in large, publicly traded companies, employee-owners collectively become just another shareholder group—another voice in the crowd. The employee ownership does little to influence the ownership level or power of the controlling owners, except in the few examples of employee-owned firms such as TWA. For ESOPs, the owner usually sees the employee purchase as a way to secure the future of the firm after the original owner's retirement, and in fact find the ESOP as a way to derive value from the firm, through its sale to employees. Where management or ownership succession within the family is not an option, an ESOP permits the SME owner in effect to sell the business to people who understand it, instead of closing it down or liquidating it for a fraction of its value.

INCIDENCE RATES AND INCIDENCE REASONS

After me, nothing—Epitaph attributed to General Charles de Gaulle.

Stock transfers of any type are exceedingly rare in SMEs. As noted above, nearly one-third of big businesses have stock transfer programs in place, with most of those being stock-option programs. Of the approximately 11 000 ESOPs in existence, 9350 (85 per cent) have been created within SMEs. The numbers of SUOs are unknown, but an informed estimate can be made. As shown in Figure 7.1, from 1994 to 2000, roughly 600 Internet related firms achieved IPO status and approximately 15 000 Internet-related firms received some form of outside financing, which was the strongest indication of the firm coming into operation.

In 1997 the number of all firms in the United States was approximately 24 million. Adjusting this number for firms in the 1994–2000 period that

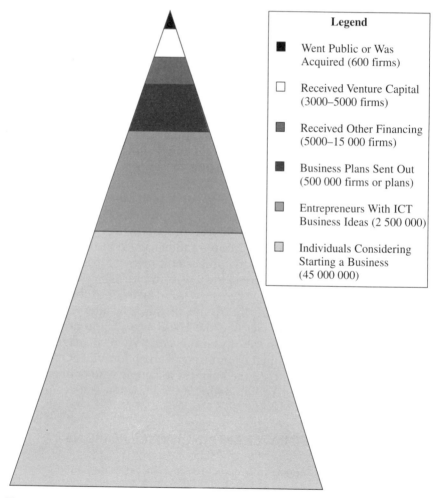

Legend

■ Went Public or Was Acquired (600 firms)

□ Received Venture Capital (3000–5000 firms)

■ Received Other Financing (5000–15 000 firms)

■ Business Plans Sent Out (500 000 firms or plans)

▨ Entrepreneurs With ICT Business Ideas (2 500 000)

▨ Individuals Considering Starting a Business (45 000 000)

Figure 7.1   The incidence of high-growth e-commerce firms in the United States (1996–2000). Sources: Jones Thompson (2000) and Reynolds (1997)

were created after 1997, or created before 1997 but ending quickly, the estimated number of firms in the 1994–2000 period is approximately 41 million. Thus, for the 1994–2000 period, the incidence rate of an American SME having an employee stock transfer plan was 0.06 per cent or *approximately 1 firm in 2000.*

Looking at the types of stock transfer in SMEs and recognizing the large number of SME firms, it becomes glaringly apparent that the key issue is why so few SMEs take advantage of any type of stock transfer approach. From the standpoint of economic logic, stock transfer makes sense. In facing the prospect of retirement or disability, SME owners arguably would need a mechanism to realize the value locked in their business and transfer or sale would achieve this. Additionally, in the United States and several European countries, there are government incentives in place to help employees buy stock in a company or even to buy a company from the owner, as a means of assuring continuation of the firm. The vast majority of SMEs around the world are family-owned businesses (Ward 1987), which means that succession of ownership is a central issue and that succession is itself a variant form of a stock option. There is even an acknowledged ownership type created expressly to assure shared stock ownership, namely the partnership, which was used in one firm out of 14 in the United States in 1996 (US Census Bureau 1999, Section 17, Table 861). Yet for all of this, the utilization of employee stock ownership within the SME is an issue that owners shy away from or neglect.

We contend that the fundamental issue is a motivational one—the drive for autonomy inherent in the self-employment situation. This motivational factor results in profound structural inhibitions that reinforce the orientation away from shared ownership. Amid this intermingling of motive and structure, the countervailing force is an orientation toward substantial wealth creation in a small subset of owners, occasionally supported structurally by distinctive practices of a reference group.

INDEPENDENCE AS THE ULTIMATE ANCHOR

I am lord of myself, accountable to none—Benjamin Franklin, *The Ultimate Success Quotations Library*, 1997.

In any analysis of SME owners, it immediately becomes apparent that the common bond among them is a desire to be independent of others—a concept widely known as autonomy. Identified as a primary need by Murray (1981), subsequent studies have found repeatedly that among business owners, the need for independence is paramount.

For example, Schein (1996) has both researched and taught entrepreneurs and managers. He has found an increasing amount of defensive self-employment where people franchise or buy a business to run to give themselves freedom and economic security after corporate downsizing, right-sizing, or early retirement. He finds those he calls entrepreneurs to be 'quite different' (p. 88) since they are more concerned about building, creating and self-aggrandizement. They take the independence to pursue their dreams as a given. In effect, all SME owners have independence as a basis, but some grow beyond this need to add desires for building.

In an update of his 1970s career anchor work Schein (1996) noted that there were eight recognized career anchors: (1) autonomy/independence; (2) security/stability; (3) technical-functional competence; (4) general managerial competence; (5) entrepreneurial creativity; (6) service; (7) pure challenge; and (8) life style. Interestingly, all the self-employed could be found holding one of two anchors—autonomy or entrepreneurial creativity.

The first anchor, autonomy, is the one that leads people to desire to own their own company and be their own boss. Those anchored in autonomy and independence seek to be self-reliant and reduce their dependence on an organization or particular job. Those anchored in entrepreneurial creativity have a slightly different set of needs. While they want to work on their own as a fundamental need, they want to create and build from the ground up. They do not want simply to own a business but want to develop it themselves in order to build new products and create new services for consumers. Presciently, Schein speculated in the late 1990s that the companies built by this group would become a major source of jobs in our society and thus we should create an economic, political and cultural environment to encourage them in their endeavors (Schein 1996).

There are numerous theories that recognize those drawn by independence and those drawn by wealth. This distinction is a fundamental and recurring one. In nineteenth-century France there was a differentiation between the self-employed speculator and the bourgeois owner (Herbert & Link 1982). In 1967, Norman Smith reanalyzed[1] the classic study of Collins & Moore (1970), finding two types he called 'opportunistic' and

---

[1] In a few cases a trichotomy has been found. The first example was one suggested by Smith (1967), but admittedly not significant in the statistical results. A more robust finding of an intermediate group was reported by Wainer & Rubin (1969) in a reanalysis of data by Schrage (1965). Moran (1998) found an intermediate group in a study of American SME owners. Using a different model for analysis, Savage (1979), using longitudinal data from France, found differences between founders, heirs, and professional managers. The dichotomy is evident in all the trichotomy studies except Savage and the number of studies finding the dichotomy are several dozen times that of studies finding the trichotomy.

'independent'. With John Miner and Jeffrey Bracker, Smith (Miner, Bracker & Smith 1989) extended this work over the next 30 years. In the 1980s, a major dispute arose in the literature over who was entitled to the label 'entrepreneur', with the resulting decision to label high-growth self-employeds 'entrepreneurs' and independence-driven self-employeds 'small business owners' (Carland et al. 1984; Gartner 1988). In the 1980s and 1990s Birch (1987) called these types 'gazelles' and 'mice'. Regardless of the labeling, the two types have been found to recur among the SME owners for more than 200 years, across industries and around the world.

We contend that the model that best describes the population of entrepreneurs is one from astronomy, called gravitational partners (Figure 7.2), like the Earth and Moon. Independence is the more massive partner, creating a type of motivational 'gravity well' drawing the vast majority of SME owners. At the other end is another smaller body, like our moon, which represents the anchor of wealth. While offering a small-scale gravity of its own, it pales in comparison with the larger base. And like gravitational partners each end influences the other (represented in Figure 7.2 by the shading within the arrows of influence), so that wealth issues can have peripheral impacts even among 'ground zero' independence-driven owners. The more common influence is that wealth-oriented types are still influenced by the desire to maintain some semblance of independence.

Wealth

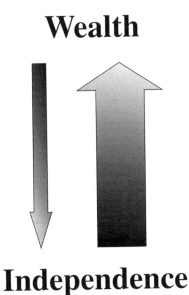

Independence

Figure 7.2   Wealth and independence orientations as gravitational partners

With this model in mind, it becomes possible to incorporate a series of studies over time that have demonstrated the presence of 'middle range' motivations, combining elements of the two gravitational extremes. The first example was what Smith (1967) called the 'technological entrepreneur', but this type was suggested but not confirmable in the statistical results. A more statistically robust finding of an intermediate group was reported by Wainer & Rubin (1969) in a reanalysis of data by Schrage (1965). Savage (1979), using longitudinal data from France, found differences between founders and professional managers, with heirs falling in the intermediate group. It is important to note that the dichotomy is evident in all the middle range studies.

CONSEQUENCES OF INDEPENDENCE

As noted earlier, the motivational gravity well of independence results in certain structural concomitants. In this section we consider three of these—organizational form, firm age, and transfer order.

Organizational Form

Independence in its purest form is most readily handled through the one-person firm (Katz 1984), also known as the quasi-organization (Star 1979) or microbusiness (Wydick 1999). Even here the two gravitational partners are evident. For a small number, the one-person firm is a starting-place for growth to a larger firm, yet for the vast majority it is the terminal form. For the former, wealth invariably plays a role in their stated goals, but for the latter, independence is paramount.

The organizational form of the one-person firm is the sole proprietorship, in which the firm and the owner are isomorphic. In virtually every nation this organizational form exists and in most nations this form represents the vast majority of firms or establishments. Even in the United States, which has one of the highest levels of corporate form and partnerships, one firm in eight is a one-person (i.e. zero employee) sole proprietorship and sole proprietorships outnumber corporations by 3.66 to one (1996 data, US Census Bureau 1999, Section 17, Table 877).

Firm Age

The drive toward independence evident in the preponderance of sole proprietorships is also evident in the way most SME owners approach issues of age. In SMEs run by their founders, firm age and owner age are inextricably linked. As Starbuck & Nystrom (1981), Danco (1979) and

Cohn (1992) noted, most firms die out with the death or disability of their owners. They reported that even 'old' firms typically die out around the quarter-century mark. This remains substantially true today. Figure 7.3 shows the percentage of firms surviving at different ages, in two-year increments. The curve is similar to the one given by Starbuck & Nystrom nearly 20 years earlier.

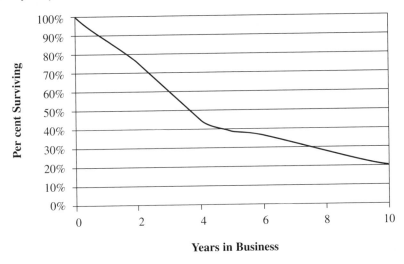

Figure 7.3   Survival rates as a function of firm age (1992–1996) (Cox & Alm 1999)

In the end, SME owners accept organizational death from 'old age' as a natural outcome. Firms that could go on are permitted to expire. For example, Table 7.1 shows that of 496 874 SMEs that died (i.e. ceased operations) in 1995, only 71 128 actually closed their doors because of business failure, defined as 'assignment, voluntary or involuntary petition in bankruptcy, attachment, execution, foreclosure, etc.' (1996 data, US Census Bureau 1999, Section 17, Table 884).

SBA statistics from the *Characteristics of Business Owners* Survey, estimated that the percentage of firms in the 1992–1996 period that were still successful at their close was 57.4 per cent for firms with employees and 36.4 per cent for firms without employees (US Small Business Administration 1998). With approximately 13 per cent of firms in 1995 having zero employees, this would suggest that over 248 000 firms closing in 1995 had employees, were still successful, and hence were candidates for some form of transfer.

There can be many reasons why transfer does not occur. In some firms, employees might not be able to carry on the business, or choose not to. The cash flow of the firm might not be sufficient to sustain a payout to the

Table 7.1   Births and deaths of SMEs in 1995

Type of statistic	Count in 1995
Number of firms, total	23 240 000
Sole proprietorships	16 955 000
Partnerships	1 654 000
Corporations	4 631 000
Firm births, total	594 369
Births of SMEs (<500 employees)	594 119
Births of firms with <20 employees	568 896
Firm deaths (1994–1995), total	497 246
Deaths of SMEs (<500 employees)	496 874
Deaths of firms with <20 employees	472 441
Firm failures (all sizes)	71 128

old owner and the salaries of the new owners or employees. Even if efforts to transfer the firm were attempted, it is possible that the process failed through disagreement on valuation or other issues. Still, the critical point is that nearly a quarter of a million firms in one year ended, while they had been successful and had employees in place. If nothing else, this represents a substantial loss of assets, not to mention loss of employment. This loss is due to 'old age' in the firm.

Independence as a drive results in self-reliance at the individual level and often in a denial of age effects in the individual or the firm. It is the nature of the independence-driven owner to do everything himself or herself. This is evident in a variety of related situations. For example, much of the research in family business planning has focused on emphasizing the need to begin succession planning long in advance of the transfer, but this has been found to be an uphill struggle (Cohn 1992). Similarly, getting most SME owners to adopt structural mechanisms that can offset the unavailability of the owner—such as business plans (Berman, Gordon & Sussman 1997) or disability insurance (Cox 1994)—have also been 'difficult sells'.

Transfer Order

As noted above in Table 7.1, the vast majority of firms die out when their owners die or retire. On the basis of American statistics from the mid-1990s, this happens even where the firm is successful and there are employees in place in the firm. It is clear that the most prevalent approach to firm ending is to close the firm, rather than to transfer ownership. Family business research (Ward 1987) indicates that the incidence of efforts to have intra-family succession is approximately 30 per cent of firms and, as noted above, the incidence of stock transfer is less than 1 per cent. This incidence rate for these successive moves from owner out to others is consistent with the expectation that most SME owners have high independence needs.

INDEPENDENCE AND STOCK TRANSFERS

What this chapter has sought to show is a series of related aspects of individual motivation and structural concomitants which collectively explain why SMEs and in particular owners of SMEs do not make use of employee stock transfer arrangements. Looking at the population of SMEs, it is clear that most owners are more likely to close down a successful, ongoing business and in effect walk away from the remaining value in their business rather than see others own it. On the surface this view appears irrational, particularly when viewed through the lens of economic rationality, but it is understandable from a psychological viewpoint.

In the preceding sections we documented how independence, the most basic of needs for SME owners, could influence decision processes and organizational structures to produce the results seen. There are also alternative psychological explanations. For most SMEs the link between the owner and the firm is profound and enduring. It is so fraught with passion that organizational psychoanalysts such as Levinson (1962), Zaleznik & Kets deVries (1975) and Kets deVries (1977) have consistently mined the dynamics of owner–firm relations and have reported that the tie is as durable and intense as those to spouses and children. In the end, most owners could no more hand over their firm to another than hand over their child.

Looked at from the perspectives of independence or psychodynamics, the actions of those who *are* able to make efforts toward organizational transfers are the ones who are distinctive within the population of SME owners. They are the rare cases, and as such require special explanations.

As noted above, the two major forms of stock transfer among SMEs, ESOPs, and SUOs, are the distinctive forms of stock transfer available to Old and New Economy SMEs, respectively. Their purposes differ from the standpoint of what they seek to offer and receive from employees and what purpose they serve for the offering owner. Neither approach is widespread in business. ESOPs are scattered thinly across industries, with succession planning the common thread, while SUOs are concentrated in the Internet-related industries, with the competitive pressures of an industry-wide practice fueling continued use of the practice.

Both approaches also depend on an orientation toward wealth creation. The purpose of ESOPs is to realize value from the business when leaving it. The alternative, as noted above, is to close down a firm, losing the majority of the firm's value in the process. The wealth purpose of SUOs has been heavily contingent upon the Internet Stock Boom, in which SUOs are used as a recruiting and retention inducement by owners of start-up SMEs. The use of SUOs replaces hard dollars and the potential of rapid capital appreciation in a booming stock market makes the possession of SUO shares attractive for new employees and SME owners both.

There is a difference between SME owners who favor SUOs over ESOPs. Moran (1998) categorized SME owners using a three-category model analogous to the one outlined above. He called his wealth anchor 'High Go', his intermediate level 'Middle Go', and the independence anchor 'Low Go.' Using an extensive battery of psychological tests, he found differences between his High Go and Middle Go owners with important implications for the ESOP/SUO distinction.

As expected based on the gravitational partners approach in Figure 7.2, both groups share an emphasis on independence, but Medium Go individuals strongly valued conformity which was ranked very low among High Go individuals. Using the Belbin self-assessment questionnaire Moran found High Go individuals to prefer being the shapers and chairmen of their organizations while Medium Go individuals emphasized working within the efficient, loyal company worker role.

Overall Moran characterizes the High Go group, which he repeatedly suggests is the entrepreneurial group, as leadership oriented. He suggests they like to set the vision for the company, be in control and make quick, firm decisions. The Medium Go owner-manager, by contrast, may have a professional or middle manager background and be more stable and conventional in running his/her business.

The Moran results help to explain the ownership orientations leading to the election of ESOPs or SUOs. For the owner creating a New Economy company during the Internet Stock Boom, the need is for fast, decisive action, assembling a team quickly and moving it toward ever higher levels of financial and technological accomplishment, with a goal of capturing wealth through being acquired or going IPO. His or her interest lies in shaping the new firm and aiming it toward wealth. The SUO becomes a quick and wealth-preserving way to achieve this while initial financial resources are scarce.

The owner of the more conventional and invariably older Old Economy firm comes with a full list of responsibilities, most notably the employees already in the firm. In seeking to withdraw accumulated wealth from the firm, the choice of an ESOP (or another internal sales approach) reflects an effort to work with those established employees and to maintain the stability of the firm and its workforce during a time of transition. Where the SUO is a fast wealth creation device, the ESOP becomes a longer-term device for transferring a firm and its existing value. It reflects and even depends on, stability to achieve its goals.

Both approaches also require substantial and ongoing planning and attention to managerial and accounting details. Both approaches require professional planning to establish the legal, financial, and accounting frameworks to make ESOPs and SUOs viable and legal, and both approaches require annual or even more frequent adjustments. This means that the SME owners electing such approaches must be comfortable with the utilization of, and even dependence on, outside consultants—a skill often hard to come by among independence driven owners.

CONCLUSION

The decision to transfer rather than close down a firm is one with profound implications for any economy. When a firm closes it doors, most of the assets and goodwill value of the firm are lost forever. The jobs that the firm provided are lost and the services or products are also lost. Amid this is also the disruption to the lives of the stakeholders of the business. The fact that literally hundreds of thousands of otherwise successful firms close down each year raises the importance of finding ways to facilitate transfers.

Ironically, even where methods exist, they are used by only the smallest fraction of SME owners. This, we argue, is due largely to a motivational outlook on the part of most SME owners that value independence more than wealth. Following de Gaulle's epitaph, these owners feel that after them, there should be no more firm. The exceptions to this 'malaise of independence' seem to hinge on SME owners whose values seem to have two bases—one of withdrawing some of the wealth accumulated in their firm, but also one of appreciation of loyalty to others and stability in their firm's operations. These three elements—wealth, loyalty, and stability—lead to efforts such as ESOPs. Blasi & Kruse (1991), looking primarily at medium and larger firms, especially those that were publicly traded, came to much the same conclusion about the orientation of the managers and directors that lead to employee stock purchase programs.

At the other extreme we see an equally small cadre of SME owners clustered in the high-technology industries, especially those related to the Internet Stock Boom, who have turned the stock offering process on its ear. Creating new firms with uncertain futures, they utilize start-up stock offerings, SUOs, as a vehicle for securing and potentially rewarding key employees. In many ways the stock being offered in such situations is speculative to the point of being 'phantom'—although that term has a special meaning in SUOs (Cohn 1992; Nesheim 2000). For these SME owners the goal is wealth creation on a massive scale and at a pace that is measured in months, not decades. It is a case of a much more focused orientation to wealth creation, with an instrumental use of SUOs to secure loyalty and have in place the team likely to secure major funding.

Indications are that ESOPs once created are generally successful at achieving the transfer of ownership and wealth (Ellentuck 1995). While Figure 7.1 above shows that of 15 000 firms with some outside funding, successful completion of an IPO occurs in only about 4 per cent of those cases, leaving more than 90 per cent of firms and employees with undervalued SUOs. This was the rate during the Internet Stock Boom and is likely to drop as the boom matures and subsides.

That said, it is still important to study the SUO phenomenon and the larger issue of increasing the rates of transfer for existing firms. SUOs have recurred periodically as a vehicle for recruitment and retention during boom times and could quickly surface with future booms around biotechnology or other as yet unknown technologies. Understanding the underlying motivations and the structural factors may help better develop, refine, and benchmark SUO practices for fast application during the short windows of opportunities boom times offer.

Similarly, looking down the road, from the perspective of the early twenty-first century, when new firm creation in the industrialized countries is at an all-time high, we face the prospect around 2025 of having a tremendous number of firms started today getting ready to be closed down. In handling the firms started in the post World War II boom, the industrialized nations have done little. The effects of loss have been largely and fortuitously masked by the ongoing expansion fueled by the growth of global trade and technology. Will our descendants be as lucky? Is there anything we can do to help? Perhaps that is the longer-term reason to improve our understanding of the underlying ideas and processes of firm ownership transfer.

REFERENCES

Aguilera, C. (1999) What A Girl Wants [Online] Available: http://gurlpages.com/christina_a_fan/lyrics.html [1 September 2000].
Berman, J. A., Gordon, D. D. & Sussman, G. (1997) A study to determine the benefits small business firms derive from sophisticated planning versus less sophisticated types of planning, *Journal of Business and Economic Studies*, 3(3): 1–11.
Birch, D. (1987). *Job Creation in America*. New York: Free Press.
Blasi, J. R. & Kruse, D. L. (1991) *The New Owners: The Mass Emergence of Employee Ownership in Public Companies and What It Means to American Business*. New York: HarperBusiness.
Bowles, M. & Sunoo, B. P. (1997) Stocks for everyone! *Workforce*, **76**(12): 24.

Burzawa, S. (1999) Labor and stock markets, tax laws, demographics influence design of executive compensation packages. *Employee Benefit Plan Review*, **54**(5): 12–14.

Cappelli, P. (1999) *The New Deal at Work*. Boston, MA: Harvard Business School Press.

Carland, J. W., Hoy, F., Boulton, W. R. & Carland, J. A. C. (1984) Differentiating entrepreneurs from small business owners: a conceptualization. *Academy of Management Review*, **9**(2): 354–359.

Chancellor, E. (1999) *Devil Take the Hindmost: A History of Financial Speculation*. New York: Farrar Straus & Giroux.

Cohn, M. (1992) *Passing the Torch*, 2nd edn. New York: McGraw-Hill.

Collins, O. & Moore, D. G. (1970). *The Organization Makers: A Behavioral Study of Independent Entrepreneurs*. New York: Appleton.

Cox, B. (1994) Myths abound about DI risks of entrepreneurs. *National Underwriter Life & Health-Financial Services Edition*, **14**: 7–8.

Cox, W. M. & Alm, R. (1999) *The New Paradigm, Federal Reserve Bank of Dallas 1999 Annual Report*, p. 3–25.

Danco, L. (1979) *Beyond Survival: A Business Owner's Guide for Success*. Reston, VA: Reston Publishing.

Ellentuck, A. B. (1995) Sell the business to your employees. *Nations Business*, **83**(2): 64.

Franklin, B. (1997) *The Ultimate Success Quotations* [Online] Available: http://www.bemorecreative.com/two/4–38.htm [11 September 2000]

Gartner, W. B. (1988). 'Who is an entrepreneur?' is the wrong question. *American Journal of Small Business*, **Spring**: 11–32.

Greengard, S. (1999). Stock options have their ups & downs. *Workforce*, **78**(12): 44–47.

Hansen, F. (2000) Currents in compensation and benefits. *Compensation and Benefits Review*, **32**(3): 6–15.

Herbert, R. F. & Link A. N. (1982) *The Entrepreneur*. New York: Praeger.

Jones Thompson, M. (1999) Recruitment spotlight: hard numbers on net executive compensation. *The Industry Standard*, 1 November. http://www.thestandard.com/research/metrics/display/0,2799,10074,00.html [1 September 2000].

Katz, J. A. (1984) One person organizations: a resource for researchers and practitioners. *American Journal of Small Business*, **8**(3): 24–30.

Kets de Vries, M. (1977) The entrepreneurial personality: a person at the crossroads. *The Journal of Management Studies*, **14**(1): 34–75.

Kirwan, R. (1999) America's best company benefits. *Money*, **28**(10): 116–126.

Lawrence, S. (2000). Recruitment spotlight: who's making those big Internet bucks? *The Industry Standard*, 31 January. http://www.thestandard.com/research/metrics/display/0,2799,10103,00.html [1 September 2000].

Levinson, H. (1962). *Men, Management and Mental Health*. Cambridge, MA: Harvard University Press.

Levinson, H. (1973) *The Great Jackass Fallacy*. Boston, MA: Division of Research, Graduate School of Business Administration, Harvard University.

McKnight, P. J. & Tomkins, C. (1999) Top executive pay in the United Kingdom: a corporate governance dilemma. *International Journal of the Economics of Business*, **6**(2): 223–243.

Miner, J. B., Smith, N. R. and Bracker, J. S. (1989) Role of entrepreneurial task motivation in the growth of technology innovative firms. *Journal of Applied Psychology*, **74**(4): 554–560.

Moran, P. (1998) Personality characteristics and growth-orientation of the small business owner-manager. *International Small Business Journal*, **16**(3): 17–38.

More workers get stock options (More Workers) (2000) *HR focus*, (00–3): 12.

Morris, C. R. (1999) *Money, Greed and Risk: Why Financial Crises and Crashes Happen*. New York: Times Books

Murray, H. A. (1981) In E. S. Schneidman (Ed.), *Endeavors in Psychology: Selections from the Personology of Henry A. Murray*. New York: Harper & Row.

National Center for Employee Ownership (NCEO History) (2000) *A Short History of the ESOP* [Online] Available: http://www.nceo.org/library/history.html [30 August 2000].

National Center for Employee Ownership (NCEO Overview) (2000) *An Overview of ESOPs, Stock Options and Employee Ownership*. [Online] Available: http://www.nceo.org/library/overview.html [30 August 2000].

Nesheim, J. L. (2000) *High Tech Start Up: The Complete Handbook for Creating Successful New High Tech Companies*. New York: Free Press.

Pratt, S. P., Reilly, R. F. and Schweihs, R. P. (1996) *Valuing a Business: The Analysis and Appraisal of Closely Held Companies*, 3rd edn). Chicago: Irwin Professional.

Proshare (2000) *Background to Employee Share Schemes and Employee Share Ownership*. [Online] Available: http://www.proshare.org.uk/eso/eso.asp [13 September 2000].

Reynolds, P. D. (1997) Who starts new firms?—Preliminary explorations of firms-in-gestation. *Small Business Economics*, **9**: 449–462.

Rodger, N. A. M. (1998) *The Safeguard of the Sea: A Naval History of Britain 1660–1649*. New York: WW Norton & Co.

Rodrick, S. (1998) *An Introduction to ESOPs*, rev. 3rd edn. Oakland, CA: National Center for Employee Ownership (NCEO). A shortened adaptation is available at http://www.nceo.org/library/history.html.

Rousseau, D. M. (1995) *Psychological Contracts in Organizations: Understanding Written and Unwritten Agreements*. Thousand Oaks, CA: Sage.

Savage, D. (1979). *Founders, Heirs and Managers: French Industrial Leadership in Transition*. Beverly Hills, CA: Sage.

Schein, E. H. (1996) Career anchors revised: implications for career development in the 21st century. *Academy of Management Executive*, **10**(4): 80–88.

Schrage, H. (1965) The R&D entrepreneur: profile of success. *Harvard Business Review*, **43**: 56–69.

Shanney-Saborsky, R. (1998) Transfers of closely held business: ESOPs and succession planning. *Journal of the American Society of CLU & CHFC*, **52**(5): 78–86.

Smith, N. R. (1967) *The Entrepreneur and his Firm: The Relationship Between Man and Type of Company*. East Lansing, MI: Michigan State University.

Star, A. D. (1979) Estimates of the number of quasi and small businesses, 1948 to 1972. *American Journal of Small Business*, **4**(2): 44–52.

Starbuck, W. H. and Nystrom, P. C. (1981) Why the world needs organisational design. *Journal of General Management*, **6**(3): 3–17.

Szabo, J. C. (1994) Giving workers a company stake. *Nations Business*, **82**(6): 54–55.

US Census Bureau (1999) *Statistical Abstract of the United States* [Online] Available: http://www.census.gov/prod/www/statistical-abstract-us.html [13 September 2000].

US Small Business Administration (1998) *Small Business Scorecard—1998*. Washington: GPO.

Wainer, H. A & Rubin, I. M. (1969) Motivation of research and development entrepreneurs: determinants of company success. *Journal of Applied Psychology*, **53**(3): 178–184.

Ward, J. L. (1987) *Keeping the Family Business Healthy*. San Francisco: Jossey-Bass.

Washington, B. T. (1925) *Up from Slavery: An Autobiography.* Garden City, NY; Doubleday.

Wydick, W. B. (1999) Credit access, human capital and class structure mobility. *Journal of Development Studies*, **35**(6): 131–141.

Zaleznik, A. and Kets deVries, M. F. R. (1975) *Power and the Corporate Mind.* Boston, MA: Houghton-Mifflin.

Index